Vertigo

The strange
new world of the
contemporary city

Vertigo

Laurence King
Publishing
in association with
Glasgow 1999

Edited by
Rowan Moore
With a foreword by
Jacques Herzog

Essays by
Aaron Betsky
Paul Davies
Brian Hatton
Stefan Leppert
Martin Pawley
Raymund Ryan
Irénée Scalbert
Deyan Sudjic
Akira Suzuki
Aaron Tan
Louise Low

The strange
new world of the
contemporary city

# Vertigo

Published 1999 by Laurence King
Publishing, London
in association with Glasgow 1999
Festival Company Ltd
Laurence King Publishing is an
imprint of Calmann & King Ltd
71 Great Russell Street
London WC1B 3BN
Telephone +44 171 831 6351
Facsimile +44 171 831 8356
e-mail enquiries@calmann-king.co.uk

A catalogue record for this book is
available from the British Library

ISBN 1 85669 153 5

Designed by Esterson Lackersteen
Picture research by Suzanne Hodgart
Research by Smith + Fowle
Gifu Housing translated from the
Japanese by Yuri Nakamura
Landschaftspark, Duisburg-Nord
translated from the German by
Susan Mackervoy

Printed in Italy

**Acknowledgements**
Thanks are due to the many talented and
dedicated people who have helped make
the 'Vertigo' book and exhibition.
Particular thanks are due, for their
inspiration, advice and forbearance, to
Aaron Betsky, Paul Davies, Liza Fior,
Jacques Herzog, Rem Koolhaas, Carolyn
Steel, Akira Suzuki and Lizzie Treip.
*Rowan Moore*

**Contributors**

Aaron Betsky is curator of architecture
and urban design at the San Francisco
Museum of Modern Art. He is
contributing editor of *Architecture*,
*Blueprint* and *ID* magazine. His most
recent publication is *Queer Space:
The Spaces of Same Sex Desire*.

Paul Davies is senior lecturer in the
architecture of tourism at South Bank
University and at the Architectural
Association, London. He visits Las Vegas,
his favourite city, as a matter of habit, or
perhaps addiction, whenever possible.

Brian Hatton is a freelance writer
based in London.

Stefan Leppert trained as a banker and a
gardener before studying landscape
architecture in Osnabrück. He is a
member of the editorial staff on the
journal *Garten+Landschaft*.

Martin Pawley is an architectural writer
and critic with a weekly column in
*The Architects' Journal.* His most recent
book, *Terminal Architecture*, is published
by Reaktion Books.

Raymund Ryan is a graduate of Yale
University and teaches at the School of
Architecture at University College, Dublin.
He is a regular contributor to journals
worldwide, including *Blueprint*,
*The Architectural Review* and *A+U*.

Irénée Scalbert teaches at the
Architectural Association, London and
is a correspondent for *Le Moniteur-
Architecture-AMC* and freelance
architecture critic for publications
including *AA Files* (where he is on the
editorial board), *The Architects' Journal*
and *Building Design*.

Akira Suzuki is an editor, critic, lecturer
and architect working in Japan. *Pacific
Edge: Contemporary Architecture on the
Pacific Rim* (Thames and Hudson) is his
most recent publication.

Deyan Sudjic established *Blueprint*
magazine in 1983. Since handing over
its editorship in 1994, he has continued to
work as a critic, curator, journalist and
writer. He is currently director of
Glasgow 1999.

Aaron Tan was born and raised in
Singapore. In 1994, he founded OMA Asia
in Hong Kong with Rem Koolhaas.
Their first group of built projects will be
completed in 1998.

Louise Low, also a Singaporean, is working
with Aaron Tan on a research project
started in 1993 at Harvard, called *Kowloon
Walled City*. She is currently the media
and research associate at OMA Asia.

# Contents

# Foreword
# Thoughts on the exhibition 'Vertigo'

Jacques Herzog

**The themes and subjects of this book are also those of the exhibition 'Vertigo', held in Glasgow in 1999. The following is a reflection on the issues raised by the exhibition.**

Many exhibition titles opt for a neutral, matter-of-fact approach, not much different from an entry in a telephone book. For instance: 'Peinture Naïve' or 'Cooking Recipes in Ancient Rome' or 'Deconstructivism'. Titles of this kind are still the rule and are not to be eschewed, for at least they make no false promises. We have an inkling of what to expect and have only ourselves to blame if we are disappointed, since the subject matter of the exhibition has, after all, been communicated in the title.

Recently, far more complicated and complex titles have come into vogue, testifying to rather ambitious intentions. They make a statement, a claim, which is to be corroborated or at least elucidated by the items on display. Many such exhibitions do not do justice to their titles. We have all had the experience of pleasurable anticipation souring into downright annoyance on discovering that the promise of the title is more shine than substance.

On the other hand, some of these exhibitions are still remembered with delight because the curator succeeded in pinpointing and

illustrating the *Zeitgeist* or revealing a new artistic position never before addressed in quite such a way. The first such exhibition that comes to mind is Harald Szeemann's 'When Attitude Becomes Form', mounted in 1969 at the Bern Kunsthalle. It may also be the very first exhibition to function as an embodiment, a *gesamtkunstwerk*, of the ideas put forward by a curator-cum-artist. Also unforgettable is Jean-François Lyotard's 'Les Immateriaux' at the Pompidou Centre in Paris, one of the few exhibitions that managed to express a philosophical position in the form of objects on display, without degrading them to mere illustrative set pieces. 'Les Immateriaux' was also of particular interest because the architectural shell of the Pompidou Centre – reputedly not the most ideal exhibition space – was for once integrated into the show and thus even acted as an enhancement.

Exhibitions on architecture pose special problems for curators because the subject matter – real though it may be, in contrast to a philosophical argument – is impossible to put on view in an exhibition space. The absent item must be conjured up in the form of impressive models, artistic drawings and eloquent plans, all arranged as tastefully as possible to stimulate the viewer's imagination. Ideally, architectural thought processes

become apparent although they can never compete with the real building and its intricate relations.

One could certainly envision 'When Attitude Becomes Form' or 'Les Immateriaux' as titles of architectural exhibitions. But 'Vertigo'? The word 'vertigo' does not have auspicious connotations. In fact, it would seem to address the sinister and even dangerous side of things: fear of heights and the attendant dizziness. Or even a double anxiety: the fear of falling passively through no fault of one's own, and the fear of responding quasi-actively to the magical attraction of the abyss and thereby succumbing to its vertiginous appeal. 'Vertigo' could be said to express an inescapable ambivalence and indeterminacy. With such a title, an exhibition, which clearly has intellectual ambitions, consciously rules out programmatic or even ideological concerns, such as those advanced by modernism.

Naturally, the title also evokes Alfred Hitchcock's famous eponymous film, in which the tension increases step by step as our uncertainty grows, somewhat like a spiral rising in reverse proportion to the pull of the dizzying maelstrom. The longer the film lasts, the greater are our doubts about the reliability of things: our uncertainty spreads like a shadow over the protagonists and the once so familiar surroundings. Gradually, every inch of the world we thought as solid as the Rock of Gibraltar begins to crumble. In the midst of ordinary, everyday life, a sense of unease arises, almost imperceptible at first, until it gradually takes shape and finally becomes visible certainty. Human relationships change with insidious subtlety, leading to conflict and ultimate catastrophe. They are not thrust upon the ordinary world from outside but come from within as latently inherent parts of the picture. Hitchcock consistently pursues what might be called a strategy of normality, whose particulars, presented with meticulous attention to ordinary details, merely heighten the suspense. One of his favourite actors, James Stewart, is the prototype of the ordinary, blameless citizen. The architectural framework is frequently middle class, sometimes even stuffy, in striking contrast to the modernist architecture often chosen as the setting for avant-garde movies by directors like Godard or Antonioni. Logically, Hitchcock rarely uses abrupt cuts and avoids estranging elements such as Godard's intentional shock attacks on the conventions of seeing.

In developing and constructing their images, artists, unlike architects, often have to resolve problems similar to those of the filmmaker. Of interest in this respect are the considerations of the photographer Jeff Wall, who often calls the oversized works he mounts in light-boxes 'cinematographic pictures'. Their radicalism rests in the very precision of an excessively constructed rendition of things that seem so familiar and ordinary. Wall himself has also indicated that he was never interested in breaks like those that occur in Godard films. He is much more involved with a radicalization of pictorial imagery within the classical form of the picture as a tableau. He consciously takes a stand in opposition to the avant garde, which by nature invites confrontation.

In the world of architecture, questions of this kind have never before been expressed and debated so explicitly. Ordinary, everyday aspects play a role at most in Robert Venturi's early writings. But since Venturi derived his notion of the everyday from popular culture, his aesthetics of the ordinary have inevitably frozen into a stylistic variation of postmodernism. 'Vertigo' is not an issue in the debate on architecture. Instead the attempt is still being made to revive the avant garde. To be avant-gardist was, and still is, the concrete yearning of the deconstructivists: the idea of a new shape never seen before that suddenly crops up from outside. Architects and critics alike are possessed with the idea, as if there were no other alternative for contemporary architecture.

But what does 'Vertigo' promise? Which attitudes will acquire shape in an exhibition of this name? Given the extreme heterogeneity of the projects and their makers, it is hardly possible to speak of a uniform formal idiom, nor of a consistent architectural approach. Nonetheless, diametrically opposed projects could conceivably come together to form a kind of imaginary city. Should the interplay of these forms, the juxtaposition of highly specific and generic architecture, reveal a fundamental tendency in our civilization? Or to reword the question: is the architecture on display capable of pointing the way to future developments or is it more like an arbitrary accumulation of individual exercises in style? Does Rowan Moore want to explore the generic in the midst of the specific and the specific in the midst of the generic? Finally, it would be conceivable to shift this heterogeneous collection of projects into one single project based on the insight that the specific grows out of work on the generic, just as Hitchcock comes up with things that are strange, frightening and, in fact, new by focusing on the familiar and the known.

© H&deM, Jacques Herzog, 1998
© Translation Catherine Schelbert

# Vertigo: The strange new world of the contemporary city

Rowan Moore

The Jewish Museum,
Berlin by Daniel
Libeskind.

Each Saturday night the people of Kuala Lumpur go, in large numbers and on choked roads, to a former quarry outside the city. Here is Sunway Lagoon, an orgy of theming, shopping and entertainment plainly inspired by Las Vegas, although gambling is prohibited and the traffic arrangements are more chaotic. Perched on the quarry's rim is an Egyptian temple/shopping mall with a giant drive-thru lion at the front that recalls the Luxor hotel's drive-thru sphinx in Las Vegas. There is a hotel pinnacled and domed like a jungle palace with more than life-size statues of elephants and panthers outside and, clinging to the sheer sides of the quarry, castles, pavilions and bits of chinoiserie.

At the bottom of the quarry, crowds stand knee-deep in a shallow lake, clapping and cheering the performers on an open stage for which the lake, and the quarry rising about it, are the auditorium. Released by the cool of the water and of the night from the humid heat of the day, the crowds are vivacious and sociable in a way in which they would never be in Kuala Lumpur proper. The way back out into the turmoil of the surrounding roads passes through a gateway surmounted by ibexes, domes and the words 'Vision 2020', a reminder of Malaysia's now creaky looking ambition to be a major economic power by the year 2020.

Sunway Lagoon is an archetype of the landscape of the present, a themed, 'imagineered', consumerist landscape that is now familiar to city-dwellers from the West End of London and the south-western deserts of the United States to the new cities of China. Sunway Lagoon is driven by shopping and entertainment; it is out-of-town, its architecture is all about creating images and it

is, as a type borrowed from the other side of the world, a manifestation of global culture. It is big and built fast. It is synthetic. Its architecture is all about creating the most explicit images possible, without any fear of looking incongruous. It aims to stimulate the spectator as directly as it can. It also aims to create a total experience, every aspect of which is directed by the management and their designers, and which makes no reference to its immediate surroundings. With its milling throngs and hubbub of voices, it looks more like the traditional idea of a city – as a hub of social interaction – than most 'real' cities do themselves.

This landscape is manifest in shopping malls, theme parks, airports, new residential enclaves and in hybrids like the themed shopping mall or the airport retail area. Each element creates a self-sufficient, artificial, all-embracing experience that is both controlled and controlling. The space between them is seen as background, as something you see through car windows when travelling from one such place to another. The soft interior of a car is itself a kindred space to the nerveless insides of shopping malls and airports, so that it becomes possible to lead life as if in a continuous, carpeted, air-conditioned tube. In all these environments, physical sensations are reduced to a minimum, and then reinstated as spectacle, as products or rides or the view through the window.

Collectively, these types are tending to create a state of global homogeneity, of universal generic space, in which identical experiences can be had in any time zone and any climate. They are hostile to the traditional idea of cities as places of diversity. Instead,

each institution tries to create its own monopoly of multiplicity, on its own terms. Inside it offers an apparently limitless choice within a fundamentally uniform experience; to the outside it offers blank façades and car parks.

Complete homogeneity is, however, a destination that will never be reached. Old, inherited fabric lingers sufficiently to contaminate the homogenizing ambitions of the new. The new, even if it aspires to uniformity, in practice reflects different ambitions, different patterns of success and failure, different customs. Even a new building has its own short history that distinguishes it from one that is slightly younger or older.

In this respect, Sunway Lagoon is also characteristic, as it is an offspring of global culture at the same time as being distinctively Malaysian. No one would be fooled into thinking they really were in Las Vegas, just as no one in the Luxor, Las Vegas would think that they really were in Luxor, Egypt. In its excess it dates itself precisely to the unbridled but just finished South-East Asian boom. More places like this will be constructed, but they will not be identical.

The landscape of the present is not therefore defined by global homogenization

In Sunway Lagoon,
Malaysia – a Las
Vegas-inspired
entertainment and
shopping centre –
imagery is borrowed
from multiple sources,
without fear of
incongruity.

but by the friction between the pressure for sameness and those awkward, inherited states that make sameness impossible. While homogenization suggests a certain boredom, the effects of this friction are, contrastingly, strangeness and incongruity of the kind that results from a colossal skyscraper being placed next to a tiny temple.

There is also a dizziness, sometimes exhilarating, sometimes frightening, that comes when the certainties on which we stand are blown away. Such dizziness is intensified by the speed, scale and sometimes height of new development. It is also created, in a more literal sense, by the devices used by shopping malls and theme parks to disorient their visitors, of which the rollercoaster is only the most extreme example. This dizziness is, by another name, vertigo.

### The architect and the imagineer
While shopping malls and theme parks are not in themselves new – although they are being built at ever-increasing scales and to ever more extreme designs – their effects on the way people live in cities, and on the role and understanding of architecture, are still rapidly evolving. Almost everything architects have held to be fundamental is now being challenged. The idea that a building should have a 'human scale' looks weak in the face of structures that – like the new Hong Kong International Airport (completed in 1998) – are the size of a Renaissance city. Classical theories of hierarchy and harmony seem ineffectual. When skyscrapers are built in Shanghai by Japanese developers and American architects, 'local character' becomes a curious concept. The relationship to nature and to the

landscape that has always been a central theme of architecture has no meaning in sealed, air-conditioned, viewless boxes decorated with synthetic trees.

For most of this century architects have argued that buildings should be 'true to materials' – that they should look like whatever they're made of – but the guiding principle of the vast majority of new development is the opposite: that neutral materials like plasterboard and glass reinforced plastic should be made to look like stone, rocks, wood or whatever else is desired. Architects want to reveal the structure of their buildings; themed space demands that it be covered up.

The argument that buildings should conform to one particular style that is appropriate to a particular time and place looks helpless in front of the promiscuity of styles of a place like Sunway Lagoon. Modernism, which tried to give itself the authority of an abstract, style-free purity, is now just one style among many. When a vernacular-style building and a modernist skyscraper stand side by side in Shanghai, or when a deconstructivist cultural centre in a European city stands next to a modernist library, neither can be said to be more valid than the other. It is hard to justify one particular shape, style, material or constructional technique as claiming a higher moral status than another. Debates about modernism versus traditionalism, or high-tech versus postmodernism now resemble the pedantic twitterings of medieval monks.

Architects want buildings to have some kind of 'integrity', some sort of fixed quality that resists change and exploitation.

Imagineers, to use a word coined in the 1980s to describe creators of fantasy landscapes for the likes of Disney, want buildings to be as subject to change, and as amenable to carrying changing images, as a television set. Imagineering's challenge to architecture is like that of nineteenth-century engineering, except that imagineering occupies the territory that architecture holds most dear: making spaces and determining their quality.

In one way architects are more powerful than ever, as buildings are being built bigger and in greater numbers than ever before, and successful architects are in demand all over the world. Norman Foster, with a global practice of several hundred people, operates on a scale no previous British architect could have dreamt of. More and more cities – Lyons, Marseilles, Tokyo – want the magic of a star architect's landmark. In another way, however, architects are more superfluous than ever, as fundamental decisions are made for them by others about the architectural qualities of their buildings. Everything is possible and everything is potentially pointless.

Architecture is no longer about finding a style or shape that is better than another, as any style or shape is equally liable to be appropriated as an image and thereby reduced to a common value. In Shenzen, China, there is a theme park with scale models of the world's great buildings – the Eiffel Tower, Venice, the Sydney Opera House and Stonehenge. Elsewhere in the city there is a working office building that looks very like Norman Foster's Century Tower in Tokyo. Whether a building is a prehistoric stone circle or a highly-wrought piece of high-tech, it has an equal capacity to become urban wallpaper.

**The builders of Shenzen, China, have no respect for architectural niceties (right). In its Windows on the World theme park (facing page, top), the world's great monuments are replicated at a reduced scale.**

A similar principle to the Windows on the World theme park operates in the city's new office buildings, where contemporary classics like Norman Foster's Century Tower are reproduced (left).

comprehensive translation of the scenography of film and television into whole buildings and environments.

This architecture creates images. As with images on a television screen, what these are made with, whether electrons or plasterboard, is irrelevant. As in a film, these images are directed and coordinated, and the viewer's role is passive. To experience them to the full you have to surrender to the fantasy. The landscape of images created by a Las Vegas resort creates its own orientation and its own bearings. The exterior is excluded to make the illusion more complete, and the surrounding context is ignored. To go from one resort to another is like channel-hopping on a television; the space between them is as neutral and irrelevant as the plastic casing of television set, or as the carpets in a cinema foyer. Or at least aspires to be so, as humanity is not so docile as to fail to give these spaces a life of their own.

Such landscapes are not entirely new, but descend via 1950s Disneyland and turn-of-the-century Coney Island from eighteenth-century pleasure gardens. What is new is the scale and comprehensiveness of these environments, and the extent of their influence into places of everyday activity, such as homes and shops.

It is clear how much things have changed in Las Vegas itself. When Robert Venturi celebrated the city a quarter-century ago in *Learning from Las Vegas* (1972), its casinos were big, bland sheds whose interiors contained slot machines lined up with industrial efficiency and one side of whose exterior became progressively engulfed by ever more extravagant neon signs. The sign, as Venturi observed, became the building. In the 1990s, in

Architecture is now about this: how do you embrace the power of imagineering, of the controlled, synthetic experience, without accepting the obliteration of the marginal, the drive to sameness, the continuous simplification of human experience that goes with it? How can a building make sense of strangeness? How can it embrace vertigo?

To misquote from Le Corbusier in *Towards a New Architecture*:
'Our imagineers are healthy and virile, active and useful, balanced and happy in their work. Our architects are disillusioned and unemployed, boastful or peevish.'

### Las Vegas, city of the future
Las Vegas is to the present what Los Angeles was to the 1960s and what New York was to the 1920s. It is a source of fascination to outsiders, who are part horrified, part awestruck. It obeys its own rules with startling indifference to other people's notions of taste, decency or public responsibility. It is imitated all over the world, and the Las Vegas-inspired theme park is as much a sine qua non of the aspiring Asian city as the gigantic skyscraper. It is the United States' fastest growing city. It is the American city people in China would most like to visit.

It is, of course, a city built on entertainment, whose urban fabric is a series of filmsets, and its power reflects that of the modern entertainment industry in which cinema and television, rather than newer media, are still dominant. The architecture of its 'resorts' – the ever-growing conglomerations of casinos, hotels, shopping malls and entertainment centres – can be seen as the ever-more

**In the 1990s, Las Vegas has seen the explosion of the themed resort with the Egyptian Luxor (right) following the Arthurian Excalibur (top). Outside Treasure Island (left), sea battles are held daily.**

New York New York
mines the melting pot
as a rich source of
theming.

a bid to attract more families, the emphasis shifted away from the former concentration on gambling towards a broader range of entertainments. As casinos became resorts, designers' efforts shifted from creating a glittering façade to making the whole building into a three-dimensional themed environment, where almost every detail, inside and out, advertises a particular theme. As a result, neon and flashing lights are now redundant. The building has become the sign.

Throughout the 1990s the new resorts became increasingly sophisticated. The Arthurian-themed Excalibur (completed in 1990) looks crude next to the Egyptian-themed Luxor (1993), which looks crude next to the New York-themed New York New York (1996), which may well turn out to be the crest of this particular wave.

The latter's genius lies in its choice of such rich subject matter as New York. Excalibur, struggling to find enough variations on its theme to differentiate its many eateries, resorts to the somewhat desperate expedient of 'Lancelotta pasta', but New York New York can draw on the whole diverse cuisine of the melting pot. Excalibur is restricted to the castle look, but its rival on the other side of Tropicana Avenue is a composite of brownstones, the City Hall, Marcel Breuer's Whitney Museum, the Brooklyn Bridge, the Statue of Liberty, the Ellis Island Immigrant's Receiving Station and, crowning the whole assemblage, a wall of ten famous skyscrapers at one-third actual size, fused together like Siamese decuplets into a single, 2,034-room hotel. Inside, apart from the usual sea of slot machines, is found a miniature Central Park with a miniature lake, a portion of Little Italy made still more little,

and plentiful art deco styling. Throughout the building, attention to detail is impressive; from the selection of authentic fire hydrants to the books, vases and toiletries displayed in the false windows of the false brownstones, to the row of bottles containing free lotions in the hotel bathrooms, which are made to look like a little skyline.

Many of the new breed of super-buildings can be compared to a city, but New York New York takes this analogy unusually far. Yet it is just as significant for the ways in which the resort departs from the original city: one of the unwritten rules of theming is that you can divorce the look of an object from the atmosphere you might associate with it. The resort is, of course, under one ownership, which has the right to decide who may or may not enter it. Its transitory residents do not, on the whole, go in fear of street crime, even though specially commissioned grafitti decorates parts of the interior. It is very clean. It is 100 per cent air-conditioned and artificially lit. It doesn't snow. When the theming lets up in the hotel corridors and bedrooms you are back in the generic space of hotels all over the world. And, looping through the whole edifice is a rollercoaster that substitutes the actual danger and uncertainty

of real city life with virtual, pre-planned, absolutely safe danger.

The geographical relationship of the many buildings to each other bears little resemblance to their location in the real New York. The relation of the external façades to what goes on immediately behind them is non-existent, and the scales are inconsistent, so that a house is made to seem the same size as the Whitney. They are plainly stage sets, constructed from indeterminate material made to resemble brick and stone, whose ornamental richness contrasts strikingly with the blunt functionality of the partly-concealed air-conditioning plant. The façades attached to the outside might imply that they lead to an interior, but the inside of the building is treated as another exterior, made up of park and street.

Clearly, no one is expected to confuse this place with the real thing, but they are expected to respond to the explicit visual cues that say 'New York', in the same way that people respond to the none-too-lifelike but immensely popular waxworks at Madame Tussauds. Successful theming borrows the associative power of the original, and the ability of images to transport you into another world. This other world, however, while camouflaged as New York or Egypt, is actually something else altogether, a place governed by the visitors' desire for escapism and simple gratification, and the management's wish to satisfy them.

Perhaps most significantly, New York New York abandons the gridded street plan of the original city. In its place it has a meandering arrangement that achieves gently what the rollercoaster does violently: it disorients

**Behind New York New York's façades is the blunt functionality of the air-conditioning plant (above). Despite the realism of the façades, scale is elastic, with the Brooklyn Bridge, the Whitney Museum and a town house all ending up at similar sizes.**

people and encourages them to move along the routes the management wants them to, which naturally means towards places where they might spend money. In this it resembles older Las Vegas casinos and, like them, removes all sense of external reality (including the time of day or weather), so that punters can immerse themselves all the more thoroughly and protractedly in the spinning world of machines.

New York New York shuts out daylight, heat and the weather and then creates its own false nature of lake, trees and rocks. It purges the city of its danger, instability and multiplicity, and reinstates them as virtual danger and virtual variety laid over an experience whose fundamentals – gambling, stage shows, eating – are not much different from those of other resorts. Having excluded external stimuli, it aims to create a complete self-sufficient experience where the stimuli are all in the control of the management.

With new resorts like the Venetian and Bellagio on the way, commentators are saying that the Las Vegas market for resorts may be (at least temporarily) saturated. New resorts will be hard-pressed to match the completeness of New York New York's theming. But, whatever happens in Las Vegas in the next few years, its values and techniques are being ever more widely applied elsewhere in the world, and to places where people live and work and spend their lives as well as where they go for their holidays.

Some of the most successful architectural practices of the 1990s are those which, like Wimberly Allison Tong and Goo (WAT&G), furnish everywhere from South Africa to Tahiti with jungle palaces, Polynesian long

houses and seashell-encrusted representations of Atlantis. Another great success of the 1990s is Jon Jerde's Jerde Partnership, who are masters at applying the techniques of entertainment and fantasy to shopping centres, public spaces and other places around the world, where they had not previously been seen.

Architects have long been fascinated by technology transfer: the application to buildings of technology invented for the space programme or the military. Now we are witnessing fantasy transfer: the application of techniques used by the entertainment industry to most kinds of building.

### Fantasy transfer

'The architecture of fantasy is not "façadomy". It cannot be applied as a veneer. Nor can it be an afterthought. The architecture of fantasy starts with a vision, a concept and a great story. Fantasy architecture turns fiction into fact. We script the experience, literally and figuratively, and then integrate the storyline into every step of the process, every facet of the program, every detail of the design.'
Wimberly Allison Tong and Goo,
*On Creativity and the Bottom Line*, 1998

For over a decade the Disney Corporation have been – as well as world leaders in the businesses of film and theme parks – leading patrons of architecture in the United States, commissioning the most famous architects in the country to design hotels, office buildings, visitor centres and the like on their sites in Florida, Los Angeles and Paris. In 1996 their contribution was honoured at the Venice Biennale of architecture, where the entire American Pavilion was dedicated to exhibiting the monuments of Medici Mouse.

In the 1990s the Corporation turned its attention to town-planning, purportedly to honour Walt Disney's dream of building a model community. The result is Celebration, a town of 20,000 inhabitants on the edge of Disney's Magic Kingdom in Florida. In keeping with Disney's architectural policy, it has a town hall by Philip Johnson, a post office by Michael Graves, a cinema by Cesar Pelli and a business park by Aldo Rossi.

It is also planned according to the principles of New Urbanism, the town planning movement that insists on such traditional urban qualities as placing homes near to places of work and giving towns a main square or similar identifiable centre. Under the rules of New Urbanism, individual

**Inside New York New York, Manhattan's brownstones and the streets of Little Italy are recreated, with a reduced risk of being mugged.**

houses have to conform to common rules that determine height, materials, colour, size of windows and the extent and nature of verandahs, fences and porticos, so that individual expression is contained within a harmonious whole. The idea is to create the sense of community and collective responsibility apparently lacking in fractured modern cities and apparently present in towns of the past. These principles have been applied to luxury housing developments in the United States, starting with Seaside, Florida (1981) and continuing with Kentlands, Maryland (1988) and Windsor, Florida (1989). They have been applied to Prince Charles's housing estate at Poundbury in Dorset, UK, and to Disney's town, Celebration.

The values of New Urbanism are in many ways admirable, and arguably preferable to those of suburban sprawl, but what Celebration makes plain is the extent to which it is also a sophisticated form of theming. Despite protestations that New Urbanism is a modern interpretation of an ancient but living tradition of city-building, developments like Celebration (and Poundbury) have as much in common with modern entertainment culture as they do with medieval Siena.

The theme at Celebration is small-town America some time before World War Two. The promotional literature is perfectly explicit about this, nostalgically evoking chats across the picket fence and other neighbourly activities believed to have disappeared around the time of Pearl Harbour. Drawings in the style of pre-war property advertisements show pre-war couples looking fondly on a pre-war house. The styles of the buildings themselves include *Gone With the Wind* southern colonial

Despite protestations to the contrary, Prince Charles's housing estate at Dorset (right) is an example of themed architecture. A *trompe l'oeil* façade prefigures the Disney Corporation's town of Celebration, Florida (below). With the verandahs and white picket fences, a bygone age of neighbourliness is nostalgically evoked.

and other variations on the classical. It gets no more modern than Cesar Pelli's art deco cinema. The individual buildings monumentalized by the famous architects – the post office, the bank, the non-multiplex cinema, the town hall – are all old-fashioned, main-street types of a kind marginalized in the age of the mall.

Celebration has another essential quality of themed space: that of being a self-contained enclave under the direction of a single private company whose rules and policy ensure the preservation of the desired image. Celebration has its own political structure and its own restrictions on anti-social behaviour, as well as being a place you have to be reasonably well-off to buy into. Despite its claims to be socially inclusive, New Urbanism has not succeeded in breaking down the barriers between those

who can and those who cannot afford to live within its precincts.

Back in Las Vegas (or, to be precise, 27 kilometres/17 miles outside), another residential enclave is taking shape. Called Lake Las Vegas Resort, it is built in the Mojave Desert around a stretch of water described as 'the largest privately owned man-made lake in the south-west.' Here, too, is a place with its own security arrangements and rules and its own Mediterranean theme, expressed in districts called Siena, Marseilles, Monaco and Barcelona, and in the evocation of the Ponte Vecchio and other ancient Italian structures in its civic centre. It is planned around a Jack Nicklaus-designed golf course, taking its shape from a sport in the same way that the Piazza Navona in Rome took its shape from a race track.

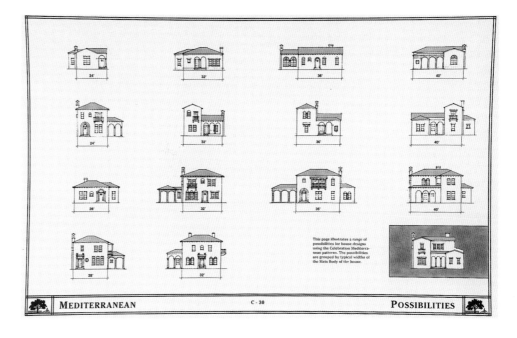

This page illustrates a range of possibilities for house designs using the Celebration Mediterranean patterns. The possibilities are grouped by typical widths of the Main Body of the house.

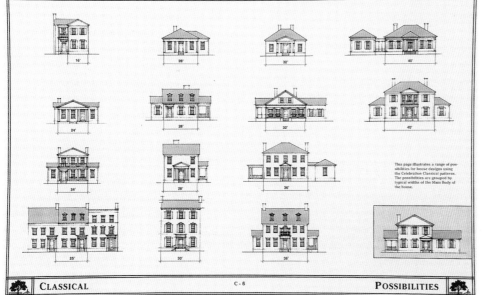

This page illustrates a range of possibilities for house designs using the Celebration Classical patterns. The possibilities are grouped by typical widths of the Main Body of the house.

At Celebration, housebuyers are offered a choice of traditional styles (above).
Each detail contributes to the overall image (right). Famous architects, such as Aldo Rossi, were enlisted to design the more monumental buildings (left).

Lot
56

Lake Las Vegas Resort is centred on leisure in the same way that the resort hotels of Las Vegas are and, like them, it creates its own artificial nature. Where the resort hotels have air-conditioning, imported trees, fake rocks, waterworks and, in one case, Siberian tigers, Lake Las Vegas Resort has created a miraculous lake in the midst of one of the most inhospitable deserts known to man, as well as improbably lush, irrigated golf courses, standing out against the lunar mountains beyond. Lake Las Vegas Resort builds on a tradition going back to the 1930s of privately owned estates that enforce their exclusive atmosphere with covenants and rules, and which, in the past, sometimes had a racist, whites-only agenda. What has changed, apart from the outlawing of the colour bar in the 1950s, is the extent and completeness of the synthetic world that Lake Las Vegas Resort creates around itself.

The similarities between resort and housing district are not accidental: one of the developers of Lake Las Vegas Resort, Henry Gluck, was also responsible for the prodigious Forum Shopping complex at Caesars World. This complex is a leader of another, spectacular, form of fantasy transfer into the retail industry. If theming and shopping have long been two of the most potent forces in the modern culture of consumption, it is only recently that anyone has realized the full impact of bringing them together. Now multi-disciplinary design teams, consisting of architects, set designers, graphic and industrial designers and lighting experts, create spaces that are as much 'storyboarded' or scripted as they are designed.

The result is places like Forum Shopping, a

**Lake Las Vegas Resort is a community built around an artificial lake in the Nevada desert. Its theming is Mediterranean.**

leader both in themed shopping and in diversifying Las Vegas away from its concentration on gambling towards other forms of leisure. Here you have the disorientating labyrinthine interior of both casino and traditional shopping mall, the same synthetic landscape and the same exclusion of the outside world. But where the design of shopping malls would once hold back at a certain point so that the goods could take centre stage, Forum Shopping engulfs the visitor with its theming. It is all ancient Rome, taking its cue from the Caesars Palace casino to which it is seemlessly joined. It is also another not-so-miniature city, with its own piazzas and squares, streets and arcades, set out under an artificial sky and periodically bathed in red by its own artificial sunsets. Its *pièces de résistance* are giant fountains, all broken

entablatures, foaming Pegasuses and naked men. The star turn is a faux-stone Bacchus, who unexpectedly moves his limbs and talks.

Another archetype of the themed mall is the Jerde Partnership's CityWalk within the Universal City complex in Los Angeles, the citadel of entertainment where they not only make films like *Jurassic Park*, but also invite the public into a theme park based on these films. In CityWalk the theme is Los Angeles itself, its streetscape and landmarks merged into an added-colour, exaggerated, safe, pedestrian-friendly version of the City of Angels for those too nervous to sample the real thing. Again, the metaphor is of a city and, again, the development looks inward and away from the real city outside.

Having started working his magic in the United States, Jerde has now completed a

**With a multiplex cinema, themed architecture and other diversions, the phenomenally successful Ontario Mills is more than just a shopping mall. It offers most of the services of a traditional town under one roof.**

The Jerde
Partnership's
CityWalk reinvents
downtown Los Angeles
in a crime-free form
(right).
The Fremont Street
Experience revives a
declining part of Los
Angeles by converting
the street into a mall-
like space (top).
CityWalk is part of the
vast Universal Studios
complex, a citadel of
the entertainment
industry (overleaf).

complex in Fukuoka, Japan, and has another planned for Shanghai. He has also designed, poignantly enough, the Fremont Street Experience in Las Vegas, a possibly doomed attempt to resuscitate a downtown that was losing out to the big new themed resorts placed ever more distantly on the Strip. Jerde's strategy was to subsume the identity of venerable old casinos like the Golden Nugget into an all-encompassing themed space, effectively making the street as much like a resort as possible.

Now, themed retail has moved from the realms of relatively esoteric places such as Forum Shopping at Caesars World, which most people would only visit when on holiday. It has migrated to the Mills complexes like Ontario Mills outside Los Angeles, where people do their more everyday shopping and entertain themselves on Saturday nights in the multi-screen cinema, and which offers under one roof – and ever more comprehensively – the services of a traditional town. Themed shopping is in part a survival strategy, as the profitability of shopping malls is threatened by oversupply, ageing building stock and the rise of internet shopping. Like popes in counter-Reformation Rome, mall magnates turn to baroque architecture in times of crisis. This strategy is, however, an aggressive and an effective one.

### Uplifting, yet different

It might be tempting to dismiss as trash the continuing rise of theming, but this would be to ignore the extent of its influence and the seriousness and professionalism of those involved, as well as the undeniable pleasure it gives. Theme architects certainly take themselves seriously, as is evidenced in WAT&G's proud rejection of 'façadomy' and their insistence, like any good modernist, on the integrity of their work. Like Mies van der Rohe, they believe that God is in the detail.

More independent observers might notice the ease with which the most honoured architectural stars, like Frank Gehry and Aldo Rossi, have been conscripted to the Disney cause. The theming boom is also attracting up-and-coming architects away from the 'art' side of the profession. Students studying under Rem Koolhaas at Harvard have developed the 'evil twin theory' that identifies the surprising similarities between the theming king, Jon Jerde, and Frank Gehry: both trained at the University of Southern California, both started their careers in mall design, both were part of the 1960s art scene in Venice, California, and both now design architectural complexes in which jagged-edged streets and piazzas are formed by irregular agglomerations of contrasting buildings.

Nor is theming confined to the mass market, as the delightful proximity on Sunset Boulevard of the House of the Blues and the Mondrian Hotel makes clear. One is a nightclub/restaurant/museum disguised as a rusty, corrugated-iron Mississippi juke joint, whose theme is contained in its title. The other is Los Angeles' coolest hotel, whose serene interiors and garden, with their surreal games of scale, James Turrell lighting installations and teasing flirtations with bad taste were put together by Philippe Starck. Both places attract queues of devotees every evening. The hotel is as much a themed environment as the House of the Blues: gorgeously themed, but still themed nonetheless.

Meanwhile, high-minded, state-subsidized, educational culture is borrowing the values and techniques of mass entertainment, with which it is in direct competition for visitors. This became particularly apparent in London in the autumn of 1996, when Segaworld, a 'virtual reality micro theme park', opened within a month of the Earth Galleries at the Natural History Museum, one of the first cultural projects supported by the National Lottery to be completed. Segaworld is dedicated wholly to entertainment and profit while the Earth Galleries are intended to educate people about geology, but they employ remarkably similar techniques. Both are inward-looking, artificially lit boxes from which an awareness of the exterior is excluded. In both, a great central escalator rises through a big circular hole to the top floor, from where visitors trickle slowly back down through the interactive, three-dimensional multimedia attractions on offer. Segaworld provides space rides or Formula One racing experiences; the Earth Galleries offer a simulation of the 1996 Kobe earthquake, dwelling rather lightly on the fact that 5,000 people were killed by it.

In the year 2000 the crossover of education and entertainment will reach its apotheosis with the £758 million Millennium Experience in Greenwich, an event which will be, according to Tony Blair, 'Exhilarating like Disney World – yet different. Educational and interactive like the Science Museum – yet different. Emotional and uplifting like a West End musical – yet different.' Here is something intended as a statement of nationhood at the turn of millennium, an equal to the Great Exhibition of 1851, which aspires to reveal

**The House of the Blues, a Mississippi-style juke joint on Sunset Boulevard.**

The Mondrian Hotel on Sunset Boulevard, Los Angeles' most fashionable hotel, offers a rival experience to the House of the Blues.

truths about the contemporary human condition, whose organizers instinctively feel that the best way of achieving these objectives is to treat the whole project as a form of spectacle. The choice of title is telling: it is not an exhibition but an experience, something which, like a 'complete entertainment experience' or a 'complete retail experience', engages the visitor's entire being.

This, it is true, is a subject of some sensitivity. On the one hand the minister in charge, Peter Mandelson, has visited both the Futuroscope theme park in France and Disney World in Florida, in search of inspiration for the Experience. On the other hand his trip to Florida caused embarrassment and ructions within the Experience management and he spent much of it making sure press photographers never got him in the same shot as Mickey Mouse. Amazingly, given the ubiquity of the mouse on his home territory, Mandelson succeeded.

The embarrassment was caused by the fact that Disney is seen as superficial and frivolous. What the Experience is trying to achieve is to use the undoubted power of Disney methods to a higher end, while attracting more visitors in a year than Disneyland, Paris. It has therefore recruited – as well as a sprinkling of 'art' architects – designers experienced in creating product launches for trade fairs and similar forms of spectacle. These designers have been assigned zones, now numbering 14 and each the size of a substantial building, that deal with subjects like the human body, spirituality, the future of work, national identity and the environment.

Within the 1-kilometre (0.62-mile) circumference of the Richard Rogers Partnership's Millennium Dome will be giant human figures, evocations of English seaside towns and rides on giant beds through three-dimensional landscapes intended to represent dreams. As in the interiors of theme parks or Las Vegas resorts, these exhibits will often be figurative in a very literal way, and be made of indeterminate materials, while allowing inconsistent scale, surprising juxtapositions and other departures from reality. Like a Las Vegas resort, the Dome makes little reference to its surroundings, in this case an industrial wasteland that was rapidly decontaminated in order to allow work to proceed.

## The new orientalism

At the end of the nineteenth century the jaded palates of Western aesthetes turned to orientalism, a fascination that expressed itself in the transfer of the graphic elegance of Japanese prints into European painting, and which was still at work in the attempts of Frank Lloyd Wright and later, Mies van der Rohe, to connect interior and exterior in the manner of a Japanese house.

In the present *fin de siècle*, orientalism has returned, this time turning its gaze on the breathtaking spectacle of modern Asian city-building. Seen from Europe, a continent so enmeshed with its past as to have come almost to a halt, there was much to exhilarate and horrify, usually at the same time. In Kuala Lumpur, the medium-sized capital of a medium-sized country, the tallest buildings in the world were completed in 1997, the first time this century that the title has left the United States. In the Pearl River Delta, China, a megalopolis of 40 million inhabitants began to form, one of whose component cities, Shenzen,

has grown from nought to three million in 15 years. In Taiwan, Hong Kong, the Philippines, South Korea, Singapore, Thailand, Indonesia and even Vietnam, office towers, residential districts and entire new cities went up in the 1990s at a speed and scale never before witnessed. Shanghai became the biggest building site the world has ever seen.

With the scale and speed of development came a disregard for urban, architectural and environmental scruples which, depending on your point of view, is either violent or liberating. To build an American-style skyscraper in a traditional Asian city can only have a drastic effect. Developers of Asian cities think nothing of clearing an entire district of closely-knit, intricate, low-rise streets – in Europe, these would be protected by neighbourhood groups and heritage legislation – and replacing them with 20 identical 30-storey slabs.

Most new Asian building can fairly be described as hideous. In Shenzen, architects challenge the sanctity of artistic authorship by trawling the world's architectural magazines and copying what they find, with due adjustment of scale, on to the elevations of their buildings. The result is a skyline in which a not-quite Norman Foster jostles with an almost-Arquitectonica and a just-Cesar Pelli.

In Manila, the Hong Kong office of the American practice HOK were asked to design a new district of 90,000 inhabitants at high speed, as the client's interest payments on the huge sum they had paid for the site were far outstripping the architects' fees. Their response was to go on a two-week tour of acknowledged urban successes, such as San Francisco, New York, Barcelona and Rome,

**The entrance sequence of the Earth Galleries in the Natural History Museum, London (left) is remarkably like that of Segaworld, which opened at the same time in the same city. The Millennium Dome, London, (right) where the crossover of education and entertainment will reach its apotheosis.**

which bore fruit in a proposal for a high-density, multi-storey, radially planned city adorned with variants of Market Street, Times Square, the Ramblas and the Trevi Fountain. For those who believe successful public spaces have something to do with both slow evolution and the genius of a place, such easy appropriation is startling.

In Shanghai, Richard Rogers was asked to master plan the financial district of Lujiazui, an area eight times the size of Canary Wharf on the opposite side of the Huangpu River from the old city centre. Rogers came up with a model of enlightened, ecologically aware city planning, with an integrated transport system connecting bicycles, public transport and cars, and which encouraged shops, homes and offices to be intermingled. Development was ordered into a giant circle, in the heart of which a was great public park.

This proposal was doomed even in its gestation, as office towers started sprouting on the site while the plan was still being drawn up. Six years later, a massive road runs through its heart, surrounded by an irregular forest of office towers. The great circus and all thoughts of mixed use or integrated transport systems have vanished, and the public open space has become a fenced-in patch of grass.

In late 1997, when asked what became of the Rogers scheme, a Shanghai planner stated, 'we implemented it, but we integrated it with elements of reality to produce a perfect plan'. The same planner, asked why elevated motorways were being run through the heart of Shanghai, said that the city had to be made more friendly to cars. Here, he added in striking contrast to received opinion in the West, bicycles are the problem, as they get in

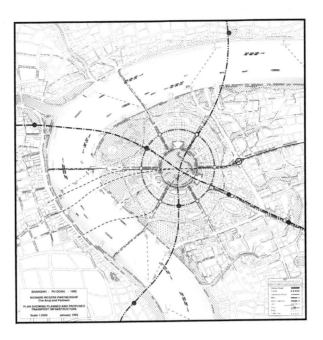

Richard Rogers' high-minded master plan for Shanghai (left) fell foul of a less ideal reality.
Almost everything in the lower picture has been built in six years. Shanghai's new skyscrapers, seen across the Huangpu River, have the same totemic presence as Communist statuary (overleaf).

the way of motorized traffic.

Now the site contains the Eastern Pearl Television Tower, the tallest television mast in Asia, whose design of pink glass spheres on a concrete stalk is meant to represent pearls dropping on to a plate. There is also the Jin Mao tower by the American practice SOM, a 420-metre (1,379-foot) stainless steel pagoda whose design makes extensive use of the Chinese lucky number, eight. On the adjacent site, a tower for the Japanese developer Minoru Mori is under construction, known either as Z-4 or the World Financial Center, which, at 460 metres (1,509 feet), will surpass the Petronas Towers in Kuala Lumpur as the tallest building in the world.

Designed by the New York office of Kohn Pedersen Fox (KPF), the tower eschews the chinoiserie of SOM for a sleek, modern look,

albeit with an oriental hint. 'The ancient Chinese conceived of the earth as a square and the sky as a circle', as William Pedersen puts it: 'The interaction between these two geometric forms gives rise to the physical form and structure of this tower. It also endows the tower with a cultural and cosmological resonance.'

In plan, the tower progresses from a square at the bottom to a long, thin rectangle at the top, producing a curved, tapering profile that is pierced at the top by a giant circular opening. The building resembles both a giant primitive totem and a twentieth-century sculpture: a Brancusi with a touch of the Barbara Hepworths. At the tower's foot is a retail mall in an irregular, deconstructivist style.

The World Financial Center is an elegant building, and according to the canons of

The Petronas Towers in Kuala Lumpur, the tallest building in the world, now look more like manifestations of political showmanship than economic success (left).

modernist good taste, KPF's abstraction is preferable to SOM's flirtation with kitsch, but in this context such distinctions count for little. What is more significant about both buildings is their sheer size, and their departure from their setting, which reflects the fact that their developers, architects and likely occupants are international.

More intriguing than its external styling is its cross-section, which reveals not only the usual office space but also a hotel with reception, banqueting, fitness club and service areas on floors 49–53 and bedrooms on floors 81–89. Around ground level is the shopping mall. At the very top are restaurants, cafés, an observation deck and a sky bridge spanning the circular opening. On the fifth floor is an art gallery developed in consultation with the Royal Academy of Arts in London. Plans for the world's highest Ferris wheel within the great circle sadly proved impractical.

Such an arrangement contains all the essential human activities of working, sleeping, eating, shopping and relaxing within a single carpeted, air-conditioned, mood-music'd enclosure, and will allow the tower to exist with the minimum possible reference to the city it dominates, in the same way that Lake Las Vegas Resort exists with the minimum possible reference to the surrounding desert. Standing in the still-unformed cityscape of Lujiazui it is, like the American, British, French and Japanese settlements that divided up central Shanghai before the war, a world sufficient unto itself.

For a while, the Asian city-building phenomenon was seen in the West as a glimpse of the city of the future. With the twenty-first century billed as the 'Asian century', and Asian economies growing by 10 per cent or more a year, structures like the Petronas Towers were seen as their political progenitors intended, as signs of economic virility. The exploding Asian cityscape of skyscrapers and shopping malls, of mass demolition and mass construction, was seen as the logical consequence of a robust free market that Europeans were too timid to emulate.

From the middle of 1997, with the successive collapse of the Thai, Malaysian, Indonesian, Korean and Japanese economies, this view has required some adjustment. It became clearer that the construction boom reflected authoritarian politics, croneyism and corruption as well as economic liberalism, and performed symbolic as well as functional roles. Thus the Petronas Towers, built by the state oil company with the encouragement of Malaysia's prime minister, now look more like manifestations of national showmanship than hard business logic.

In China, the explosive growth of Shanghai and the Pearl River Delta owed much to the fact that they are Special Economic Zones – geographically small areas where capitalism is given a special dispensation to flourish – separated from the rest of the People's Republic of China by fiercely maintained borders. Here, too, skyscrapers act as icons as much as things of use, as glorified in propaganda posters as tractors and peasants once were, and rising over cities with the same totemic power as giant bronze statues of revolutionary heroes. The skyline of Shanghai, much of which is unoccupied, seems to represent a great world city, which it is not, but may some day become.

After the crash, the Asian city of the 1990s looks more like an extraordinary, explosive historical moment than the future destiny of the world, but it is barely less impactful for that. It may no longer seem based on logic, but it is undeniably still there. It presents a vision of the city with its own seemingly inexorable will, which is also in some sense horrifying, so indifferent does it seem to notions of an individual or local identity, or continuity with the past, and so materialist in its motivation. At the same time, the instinct to recoil is checked by the knowledge that great cities of the past, whether Rome or Chicago or London, were built with comparable avarice, brutality, showmanship and recklessness.

For Westerners, the fascination with Asian cities is perhaps reinforced by atavistic racial myths, such as the inscrutable, cunning genius of the Chinaman, his ant-like numerousness, and his alleged ant-like ability to act as part of gigantic, single-minded horde. The fascination is further intensified by the fact that modern Asian urbanism is largely Western in its inspiration or, to be more precise, American. It holds up an enlarging mirror that reflects a landscape of giant office buildings, car-based planning, shopping malls and themed spaces, its creation driven by big financial institutions and corporations. We know this landscape very well, but no one in Europe or even America has the nerve to pursue it as ruthlessly as this. Of course, the Asian financial crisis might well turn out to be a stumble rather than a fall in the onward progress of the region. In which case what we have so far seen is only the beginning.

**In Shanghai, housing developments like Sun Wonderland have nothing in common with the intricate, low-rise streets they replace, a fact apparently celebrated by this out-of-scale montage (right).**

The Shanghai World Financial Center with its oculus and observation deck at the top of the tower (left).

Shanghai's planners are thrusting motorways through the heart of the city with a ruthlessness that Western planners no longer countenance (right). The city's new towers rise into the smoggy air (far right).

## Death by carpet

In contemporary construction, certain themes recur across building types and across continents. In particular, there is the idea of the substitute city, the big, all-inclusive environment that, whether it is a skyscraper, a leisure centre, a shopping mall or a residential district, aims to supply all needs, create its own artificial nature and its own synthetic experience, and cover every eventuality, all on its terms. In order to work it needs to separate itself from its context, and anything external that might provide a rival experience.

The temporary citizens of the substitute city are disoriented, whether violently by a rollercoaster or gently by labyrinthine planning and irregular architecture, or by the denial of normal expectations of scale. They are seduced by spectacle. They experience two kinds of space, seemingly opposite but actually complementary: the generic, which suppresses awareness of difference, and the themed, which fills the void with manufactured difference.

In such environments, the material, structure and underlying form of a building are awkward reminders of an alternative reality, spoilers of the illusion like the strings of a puppet, and are, along with natural light and ventilation, downplayed. The spatial ideal is a television set, a neutral container for spectacle.

This is a world that big business finds congenial and tends to encourage, as it reduces awkward differences and unpredictable appetites, making the consumer more susceptible to manipulation by the mass market. The value of the substitute city is that it protects its owners against events outside

their control.

Given the march of theming and the wholesale import of American building types into Asian cities, it is easy to fantasize that the world will soon consist of a single type of generic space, the tedium of which is relieved only by the synthetic revelry of the themers. We will all live, it might seem, in a global hotel lobby or convention centre where national differences will be reduced to the clips of pointy-hatted, hands-together Thai dancers, or British guardsmen, or tangoing Argentines, which CNN plays in its commercial breaks. We can expect to be cheered up only by the pianist playing *The Entertainer* over by the big flower arrangement, or by the rollerblading female saxophonists laid on by the drapery importers in Hall C6.

Many business people already inhabit this

world: the office–car–airport–aeroplane–airport–car–hotel–convention centre sequence is effectively a journey through one kind of space which the night off in a colourful bar in the old quarter hardly alleviates. It is a world that has decreasing use for anything as embodied as architecture, or as complex as a city, and whose coming into being, apparently, can only be accelerated by the continuing rise of electronic technologies.

These technologies separate images and information from their material presence, and make geographical proximity irrelevant, thereby bypassing the physical basis of architecture. Their use of architectural metaphors – 'windows', 'gateways', 'architecture' – serves only to emphasize how un-architectural electronic space is, as there could be nothing less like a real window (the kind that admits and modulates light) than the multicoloured graphic window invented by Microsoft.

The computer industry is also generating a distinctive architecture, which can be seen in both the Microsoft headquarters in Seattle and in the fabled Bill Gates mansion outside that city. To be more accurate, it is distinctive for its lack of distinction, its startling banality. The mansion famously has the ability to flash the world's artistic masterpieces on the wall, and to pursue visitors round the interior with their favourite tunes, but in strictly architectural terms this electronic Xanadu looks like an ordinary suburban home, much enlarged. It is the equivalent of a computer terminal, whose dumb beige exterior contains a wealth of imagery and information greater than that of the ancient library of Alexandria.

So it is with the rows of X-blocks placed

**In Microsoft's headquarters (above and far left), as in Bill Gates's mansion (left), the wealth of information inside is belied by the banality of the exteriors, which are the architectural equivalents of the beige casing of a computer.**

within the low-density citadel of the electronic industry, Microsoft's headquarters, which resemble cell blocks in a modern prison. So it is in Cyberjaya, the would-be city of the future planned in the jungle south of Kuala Lumpur. It was planned that this city would have its own cyberlaws and its own cybercurrency, and be served by fibre-optic connections of unprecedented amplitude, but its architecture, insofar as it exists at all, is low-rise indeterminate stuff of the kind found in business parks.

But we have not yet succumbed to this world of infinite carpet. All the world is not yet a theme park, not even remotely. Today's cities are characterized, not by the universal triumph of generic space, but by the often dramatic encounters between the generic and the specific; the global and the local; the slick present and the recalcitrant past. A Cesar Pelli skyscraper in Kuala Lumpur is different from one in London or New York by virtue less of its variations in external treatment than of its significance within a given context. No matter how drastic the rebuilding of Shanghai, it is taking place within a fabric undoubtably shaped by the past.

Similar encounters are unfolding in less dramatic form everywhere. In western Europe, for example, the American road-culture of big-shed, out-of-town shopping centres and entertainment complexes has infiltrated the continent's network of towns and ex-industrial cities, but is far from making the latter disappear. Even young places – Shenzen, say, or Las Vegas – have their own strangeness and their own complexity arising out of the specific conditions of their making.

These encounters produce what are actually the distinctive moments of the contemporary city: the hybrid space, the strange juxtaposition, the sudden shift in scale or variation in intensity, incongruity. Its more obvious manifestations are the coexistence of IKEA and the hand-carved Hindu temple on the North Circular Road in a suburb of London, or Christmas decorations in Communist Chinese cities, or the many different imitations of Las Vegas in different parts of the world, or skyscrapers standing next to shacks, or golf courses next to desert, or the simultaneous construction in Dresden of an avant-garde cinema complex and a replica of the baroque Frauenkirche, or the appearance at Canary Wharf of a fully functioning, self-sufficient, American-style financial centre in the middle of industrial dereliction.

There are also large-scale attempts to assert local and national identity and to create alternatives to generic space, manifest in the urge of many government bodies to employ famous architects to build new cultural institutions to adorn their cities. It would be simplistic to say that such attempts are always successful, but the intention is there and is at least sometimes fulfilled.

As city centres are seen to be threatened by the growth of substitute cities, these assertions of identity usually coincide with the need to reinforce the presence of a traditional city. In some places, where high streets are losing business to giant shopping complexes, the threat is real. In others, city centres are more often simply adjusting their role. They are becoming one centre among many, offering diversity and complexity – that substitute cities cannot.

### The virgin and the whore

Architects now find themselves in an ambiguous position. On the one hand new buildings are bigger and more numerous than ever before, and architects can now do, technically speaking, almost anything they want. They have at their disposal high-performance materials and engineers who can fulfil almost any whim. Computer drafting makes the most outlandish shape conceivable. The technology of mimicry and replication, did they but use it, has reached new heights. Thanks partly to the themers, the possibilities of what a building can be and looks like have been blown open, and a world in love with spectacle demands spectacle from its buildings. Mayors and presidents beg architects to be the saviours of their cities.

On the other hand, they face a culture that regards as obstacles precisely those things that architects equate with integrity, like the honest expression of materials and structure, formal coherence or sensitivity to context or landscape. The very range of possibilities makes the choice of any one almost meaningless, so the adherence to a particular style, through which architects used to give themselves a sense of identity, becomes cranky. To declare yourself a modernist or a classicist is to make an empty boast. Indeed, to adhere to a particular look is to make yourself prey to a culture that lives off the rapid consumption of imagery, which can make the most serious-minded artistic creation into a fashion statement

A place like New York New York, or Lake Las Vegas Resort, or the World Financial Center in Shanghai, or a Jerde shopping mall, is architecturally powerful, and makes its

**The incongruous – like the appearance of a hand-carved Hindu temple on London's North Circular Road – is a distinctive characteristic of the contemporary city.**

developers rich and its users happy. It attracts impressive resources of money and talent, and its makers are professional and imaginative. Some exhibit the freedom to think anew, to do the unprecedented, which is one of the hallmarks of great architecture. Some will undoubtedly become revered landmarks in the future. To oppose them, to say that they shouldn't exist, is unreasonably puritanical and quixotic.

Yet these places also arouse disquiet; a sense that something important is lost in their obliteration of the marginal, that there is more to life than their synthetic, controlled environments. They contain a simple social problem, which is that the pleasures of these places are not available to people who can't afford them. There is, in addition, a more complex human problem, which is that they reduce all the richness and uncertainty of human experience to the pressing of a few predictable emotional buttons. Architecture finds itself between resistance and complicity, or virginity and whoredom, which has been, in fact, its habitual position throughout history. If architects affect moral purity, they tend to become irrelevant, a little ridiculous and, worse, unemployed. If they simply produce environments exactly as their clients would like them to be, they are failing to recognize their wider responsibilities to the societies in which their buildings are placed.

In practice the title 'architect' covers everyone from Lebbeus Woods, designer of beautiful but unbuildable dreams, to Wimberly Allison Tong and Goo, whose philosophy was formed by its founder, George 'Pete' Wimberly: 'the value of good design – what a building looks like and how it feels to people – can be rung up on a cash register.' Talented and honourable people spend their lives working at these extremes, and at every point between them. It could not be otherwise. But at least some members of the profession have to work in a way that combines creative independence with effectiveness, if architecture is not to be either a picturesque irrelevance or a sub-discipline of accountancy. This in turn means understanding the shifting landscapes in which architecture takes place, and developing new strategies in response to them. To be effective, such strategies have to embrace the power of theming and other forces at work, without accepting their values.

**The marks of genius**
If architecture as traditionally understood is threatened, it is also accorded an unusually high political value. Or at least architects are. The cult of the star architect has never been stronger, and figures like Santiago Calatrava and Richard Meier are invited to travel from city to city, becoming purveyors of landmarks to needy mayors. Governments and corporations compile teams of them on which the same names frequently recur: Piano, Rogers, Foster, Libeskind, Kollhoff, Jahn and Gehry in Berlin; Gehry, Foster, Calatrava, Stirling/Wilford and Pelli in Bilbao; Meier, OMA and Graves in The Hague; OMA, Botta, Farrell, Sottsass and Nouvel in Seoul; Foster and Calatrava in Valencia; Meier, Foster, Hollein, Ungers, Behnisch and Peichl in Frankfurt; Meier, Foster, Gehry, Calatrava, Isozaki, Miralles and Bofill in Barcelona.

These architects are asked to design landmarks like bridges or communication masts, objects whose relatively simple, functional requirements nonetheless require a degree of constructional athleticism, which the architect can turn into a striking spectacle. They are asked to design railway stations and airports, or at least the elegant roofs that cover the lasagne and spaghetti of intersecting functions laid out by transport engineers and retail planners. As with bridges, everyone can see what the architecture is for, while the engineering issues are sufficiently challenging to provide the pretext for a display of bravado.

Other popular commissions are convention centres, town halls, parliament buildings, master plans for public spaces and reviving new quarters of the city. The most popular, however, are cultural buildings and museums, in particular art galleries, which have proved delightfully malleable to the imagination of architects. The fly towers and auditoria of theatres and opera houses can prove a little awkward to mould into new shapes, but the space for exhibiting art can, in theory at least, be almost any shape. Amazingly, given the public's usual opposition to apparently frivolous public spending, and to supporting minority cultural interests, these projects generally attract little effective opposition.

These commissions allow architects to stress the architectural qualities of their buildings, where 'architectural' means expressed structure and coherent form, the sort of things found on the Parthenon in its present, ruined state, and the sort of things that a retail designer would suppress. An architect like Calatrava makes a kind of frozen ballet out of the structure of his building, expressing the forces at work with exaggerated curves and arabesques. There is

**Coop Himmelblau's avant-garde cinema complex in Dresden was built at the same time that a computer-assisted reconstruction of a baroque church was started in the same city. Both projects could be described as 'contemporary'.**

showmanship in his work, but there is no disguise: what you see are the spars and wires that really are holding up the building. They are, to use the metaphor of an architect fascinated with animal skeletons, the bones of the building.

In Richard Meier's work, everything is done with the fundamental elements of architecture: posts and beams, curved and straight walls, window-like openings, ramps and stairs and basic geometrical forms, left free of decoration and colour for greater emphasis. The fact that many of these elements are not performing a functional purpose, but are simply framing a view of the sky or forming part of the composition, only serves to emphasize their role as icons of architecture.

Both Calatrava and Meier then recombine and reshape these irreducible elements according to the laws of their own genius. These laws are inscrutable and resistant to logical analysis, which they have to be if they are to retain their status as the unique marks of an artist. At the same time they must be consistent, so that they can be recognized wherever they appear. They must also be pervasive, informing or influencing every part of the building. Even though a modern architectural practice can be hundreds strong, its products must be seen to emanate from the imagination of one person.

Coloured white for greater purity, a Calatrava or a Meier building aims for a level of structural and artistic integrity that makes addition, subtraction, change or adaptation impossible, except perhaps by the architects themselves. They have the whited timelessness of a tomb or, in Calatrava's case, a

**A star architect like Santiago Calatrava produces athletic structures to which nothing can be added or taken away. Lyons Train Station, France (above and overleaf).**

skeleton. Their relation to their surroundings is always one of detachment: an elegant bridge lightly touching the post-industrial scrubland of Salford or Seville (Calatrava); the pristine museum of contemporary art in Barcelona standing out against the crumbling, brown, washing-strewn tenements of the Barrio Gotico (Meier).

They are buildings designed primarily for natural light – something which is the same now as it has been for millennia – rather than for the transient effects of artificial light. They eschew the services of imagineers, scene-setters, shopfitters and interior designers, confining themselves to those effects – the fall of natural light, the play of materials and form, the organizing of spaces – that can be directed by an architect.

Calatrava and Meier are not alone. The themes of architectural and artistic integrity underlie almost every well-known modern public building. In Paris the best known *grands projets* are those that make individual elements – an arch, a pyramid, four towers – into the beginning and end of their architecture. The astonishing international success of Norman Foster comes from his judicious combination of structural integrity and a consistent artistic style, with professionalism in the delivery of the product. Other architects, like Gehry and Miralles, produce buildings whose apparent denial of conventional building logic serves to underline their imaginative power.

In Britain, the wave of major public projects funded by the National Lottery (the plain mediocre ones apart), fall into two main categories: structural ballet by high-tech architects, and expressionist displays of wilful creativity by Daniel Libeskind, Michael Wilford and others. A really successful Lottery architect, such as Nick Grimshaw, combines both. Expressionism is also fast becoming the standard civic style of Britain's cities, as Miralles' commission to design the new Scottish Parliament confirms.

The fascination with these architects is like modern culture's fascination with both the athlete and the personality, with the unfakeable, masterful, unrepeatable, individual performance that stands out in a world of illusion and simulation. Performing in the clear light of day, these architects give themselves nowhere to hide, so their every movement is, like an athlete's, subject to scrutiny. Less their task should be too easy, they increase the factor of difficulty by suspending and cantilevering their structures, or setting themselves record-breaking tasks such as constructing the tallest, fastest, widest spanning, largest, lightest or even the most expensive structure.

The new Hong Kong International Airport at Chek Lap Kok is such a building. It was built for political as well as practical reasons, as a statement of faith by the outgoing British administration in Hong Kong's future and as a way of tying up Hong Kong's capital in something that, unlike more fluid assets, could be neither filched by Beijing nor spirited abroad during a bout of jitters. After some haggling, its existence was written into the agreement between China and Britain on Hong Kong's handover; some observers suggest that the People's Republic deliberately delayed agreement to ensure that the opening of the prestigious structure would take place under their rule.

The airport is also Hong Kong's entry in a regional contest to create South-East Asia's leading airport, which has seen the construction of magnificent structures in Kuala Lumpur, Osaka and Singapore, and the planning of others in Shanghai and Seoul. Singapore airport, its interior rich with fountains, marble and ornamental fishtanks, is an object of such national pride that a continuous line of school parties (in crocodiles; boys in blue shorts, girls in red shorts) can be seen snaking through its halls.

For their architect, the Hong Kong authorities turned to Sir Norman Foster, as they had when planning an earlier confidence-building structure, the Hongkong and Shanghai Bank. Foster's job was not to design the artificial island on which the airport was built; nor the new city built nearby; nor the railways, roads and bridges that would connect the airport to the city; nor the business centre, hotels and support buildings attached to the airport; nor even to plan the passenger flows, baggage handling and retail areas of the passenger terminal; but to design the terminal's superstructure, on a layout previously worked out by others. This superstructure, although visible from space, is only part of a gigantic whole. It does, however, determine the public perception of the building, which is why Foster is credited as the designer of the airport.

Below Foster's roof is a world of great organizational complexity; eight teaming storeys in a constant state of accretion, adaptation and demolition. It is a place with at least some of the attributes of a city, and includes the world's largest duty-free shopping mall, with all the transience,

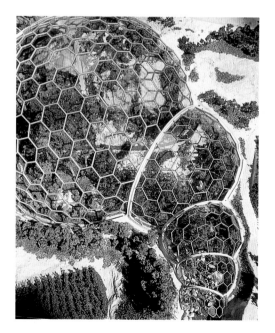

Enric Miralles' commission to design the new Scottish Parliament confirms expressionism as the new civic style of Britain (right). The projects most favoured by Britain's National Lottery combine expressionism with structural drama – like Nick Grimshaw's Eden Centre, Cornwall (left).

gaudiness and lack of conventional architectural good taste that this implies. The roof displays heroic indifference to all this, standing as a piece of unchanging architectural purity, its symmetrical plan comprised of rhythmic bays, exposed structure, consistent details and serene grey-green light. It is like an elegant CD player that retains its dignity in spite of the perfectly visible wires spewing from its back.

Around the roof's perimeter snakes the world's longest glass wall, allowing natural light (which architects like to see as the guarantor of proper architecture) into the synthetic maelstrom of the lower levels. The roof is traditional, almost Victorian in its basic concept, but is realized at a scale and speed and structural leanness that required the engineers Ove Arup to use the most sophisticated computer-generated structural models. It therefore fulfils the requirement of high-level athletic performance. It also has its expressionist touches, the roof swooping up and down along its 1-kilometre (0.62-mile) length as if in flight.

Without denigrating the technical complexity of Foster's superstructure, this temple built on an anthill should nonetheless be seen primarily as a monument. There is something quixotic about its assertion of stability in the face of flux, although it is hard to know what architectural strategy would have worked better.

### The urban Rolex

If public buildings by cultural architects set themselves up in opposition to the values of shopping and theming, of the cultures of consumption and entertainment, they cannot

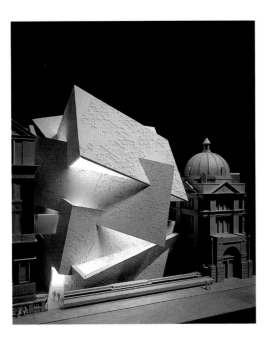

completely avoid the latter's influence. The separation of public and private worlds is not absolute. If an ostensibly commercial structure like a skyscraper can turn out to have a political purpose, a public building can also have a commercial function and display the properties of commercial architecture.

If star architects are cultural athletes they are also, like athletes, marketable commodities. Their commissioning by cities and institutions is a form of shopping, the acquisition of urban Rolexes from a limited range of known brand names. It is a form of advertising, where buildings perform the role of three-dimensional, international, permanent advertisements for a city. It is also a form of theming, in which politicians deploy well-known symbols to create an image of themselves as an enlightened, forward-

looking city.

Architecture, in other words, is treated as a commodity or product, which makes it essential that the architects concerned stick to their brand values and brand identities. Hence the whiteness of Meier, the skeletonism of Calatrava, the waywardness of Gehry. An architect's signature style – the mark of his artistic integrity – is also the very thing that makes him (and it is almost never 'her') into an object of trade.

These signatures are further exaggerated by the need for spectacle that is fed by the modern entertainment industry. In a world where the special effects budgets for a single film could buy a large building, and where Egypt and New York are lavishly recreated in Las Vegas, reticence and subtlety are falling stock. The cultural buildings of today are more dazzling, more startling, more outlandish, more in search of the 'wow' factor than their equivalents 30 or even 10 years ago. Gehry has succeeded Kahn; Rogers has succeeded Lasdun and the Smithsons. Stirling's Staatsgallerie in Stuttgart, which seemed so outré when it opened in 1984, now seems almost studious.

Nor are the buildings that these architects design entirely innocent of the qualities of consumer culture. To the extent that it is a place for visual browsing, an art gallery is not so very different from a shopping mall. Indeed, it owes its very popularity to the fact that, unlike theatre or opera, it requires very little conscious adjustment of everyday urban behaviour. Cultural buildings are also becoming places of consumption in a more literal sense, acquiring ever larger shops and restaurants, and franchising products sold off the premises.

**Daniel Libeskind's spiral for the Victoria and Albert Museum, London, will, if built, be another example of expressionist architecture in Britain (top). Norman Foster's superstructure for Check Lap Kok Airport is a thing of use, but also a political symbol of faith in Hong Kong's future (right).**

The Getty Centre in Los Angeles is a case in point. Here is a place built by the colossal legacy of a legendary millionaire, whose purpose is to enrich with art the lives of those who visit it, and to make accessible to the public visual experiences more profound than they might encounter in their daily lives. The building, constructed at great expense and to the highest standards, was designed by Richard Meier who, at the time of his appointment in 1983, was widely considered to be the greatest architect in the world and whose reputation now is not exactly modest.

The Getty Centre is full of geometrical manoeuvres and abstract forms announcing its seriousness as architecture. It evokes the Mediterranean city, the classical villa, the Greek Acropolis. It drips with a gorgeous, honey-coloured travertine extracted at great expense from Italian soil. It is massive, permanent and undecorated, the opposite of the trashy, transient, sign-laden city of Los Angeles. It is a beautiful place, cooled by ocean breezes and standing on a wooded hill above a breathtaking view. It is somewhere you can indeed go to refresh the spirits with art.

But it is also a theme park, albeit a high-class one. Like a theme park, it is a self-sufficient compound placed at a distance from the city centre (despite the popular view that Los Angeles has no centre, there are areas that are more central than others). From the moment you enter the car park, with its pleasantly high ceilings and its decks colour-coded in mauve and lilac, you are in a world where every detail conforms to a theme, which in this case is 'good taste'.

Taking a lift from the car park brings you to a white railway station whence a little white

train (reminiscent of the trains that connect Las Vegas casinos under the same ownership) takes you to the town square at the heart of the Getty's substitute city. From here on the consistency of Meier's architecture, its use of a very few details and a very few shades of white and off-white, sustains the theming. So too does the fact that this work of a New Yorker looking to Italy is so unlike Los Angeles. Anything that might remind you of alternative forms of reality is treated as background, as something in the distance, as a view.

It may not be so terrible that the Getty is like this. Some have argued for a museum more engaged with the gritty realities of Los Angeles, and more accessible to all levels of its population, but a case can be made for the Getty's escapism, and for making available to the public a piece of real estate in an area

usually available only to the super-rich. It's not that the themed quality of the Getty is corrupting; it is just the way it is.

More questionable is the rebuilding of central Berlin, an operation that has enlisted more of the world's most distinguished architects than any other, and which seems concerned with bringing back to life the devastated heart of a great European city. It is not just a question of building museums and landmarks, although there are plenty of these, but also a parliament, avenues and squares, embassies, government offices and all the architectural trappings of the capital that Berlin will soon once again be.

This rebuilding has been the subject of heated debate, focusing on the area of central Berlin obliterated by wartime bombing and the construction of the Wall, and in particular on Potsdamer Platz and Leipziger Platz, the old centres of Berlin life that had completely disappeared. As Daimler-Benz had purchased a large area of this land shortly before the Wall came down, and was keen to develop it, the issue was of more than theoretical interest.

The debate turned on the the the city government's desire to reinstate the street plan and block pattern of nineteenth-century Berlin, which had survived in the area up until World War Two. They also insisted that the detail of new development should follow a nineteenth-century pattern, with buildings conforming to a consistent cornice line and presenting to the streets predominantly masonry walls with punched-out, classically proportioned windows. Unfortunately, the stripped-down classical architecture that results from these strictures often recalls the totalitarian buildings of Berlin's Nazi and

**With its high quality materials, hill-top setting and abstract architecture, Richard Meier's Getty Centre is the opposite of the rest of Los Angeles (above). With its own railway, it is a self-contained world, bearing the same relation to its surroundings as a theme park or shopping mall (right, and facing page).**

Communist regimes.

This policy was promoted in the name of history, but its actual effect would be to suppress one history in favour of another, burying the traces of recent trauma – the Wall and bomb damage – beneath an image of a unified, harmonious Germany at peace with its past. To its critics, it is denial practised at an urban scale, an attempt to pretend that the last 60 years hadn't happened. Why a city with Berlin's history should be so nostalgic about its past as to recreate its architecture is another pertinent question.

The resemblance to old Berlin, moreover, is strictly in the realm of shape. The traditional Berlin city block is a place where multiple interests – flat dwellers, shopkeepers, owners of small businesses – can form a community focused on the block's courtyard. A modern Berlin block is the property of a single multinational company, its courtyard glassed over to become an atrium. The original Potsdamer Platz was a centre of café society, and its fabric was also the creation of multiple competing interests. The new one will be a forecourt for the gigantic new Sony Centre.

The proof that real history is being translated into virtual history can be seen with particular clarity at the Brandenburg Gate. Standing alone on the frontier of East and West, the Brandenburg Gate was one of the most potent historical symbols of recent times. Now the square in which it originally stood, Pariser Platz, is being approximately reconstructed, with a consistent cornice line, stone façades and other regularizing aesthetic rules. Within these, the celebrated architects who are designing the buildings that make up the square struggle to express their individuality with arbitrary variations in the elevations. Nearby, the reconstructed Hotel Adlon offers a synthetic, international hotel chain image of old Berlin life. The Gate itself, standing on something more nearly like its 'correct' setting, has lost much of its symbolic power, and is now a monument to art history rather than history.

The exception to this urbanism of forgetting is Daniel Libeskind's Jewish Museum, more properly known – thanks to the intricate sensitivities associated with its nomenclature – as the Extension of the Berlin Museum with the Jewish Museum Department. Conceived before the Wall came down, it was almost abandoned as a result of government spending cuts, until the authorities were shamed into letting it through.

Here is a building dedicated to enshrining the terrible complexities of Berlin's history, to ensuring that its past can never be smoothed over. It takes as its theme the central problem of representing Jewish culture in Berlin, which is this: given that the Jewish population of Berlin was the most integrated in Germany, how do you represent their culture without also confirming the Nazi view of Jews as a race utterly apart? On the other hand, if Jews are shown as Berliners like any other, how do you not belittle the terrible historic events that set them apart?

Libeskind's building embodies this dilemma without attempting to resolve it. An extension to the baroque palace housing the Berlin Museum, it is both umbilically linked to it and, in every aspect of its jagged external appearance, completely different from it. Inside the extension, exhibits will show the contributions to Berlin life by Berliners who were also Jews, while a void space cutting through the exhibition areas acts as an image of the gap left in Berlin by the destruction of its Jewish population. Everything about the building defies easy consumption: its lack of conventional hierarchy or symmetry; the enigmatic slashes and ciphers that it has for windows; its sloping floors; its uningratiating zinc and concrete finishes; the fact that its zigzag shape cannot be comprehended from any one point at ground level; the absence of a visible front door; its large areas of blankness. Yet it is not an ugly or a depressing building, but one possessed of its own strange beauty.

It's not that Berlin should be expected to live in a state of permanent angst about its past. It may even be that there was little realistic alternative to allowing multinational businesses to lead the redevelopment of Berlin's centre. What is alarming is the way in which supremely talented architects have been conscripted, in the name of culture, history and the public's benefit, to create virtual culture and commodified history in the service of the corporate good.

## Art and fashion

Architectural integrity is a protean thing. The moment that it becomes too closely identified with a particular approach, a particular combination of materials or forms, or a particular theoretical position, is the moment it becomes a marketable commodity, an 'ism', a fashion statement. Yet if architects attempt to exist in a pious world uninfluenced by fashion or the market, they will not only be unemployed and ineffectual, they will also fail in their central ambition. Consumerist culture

**Daniel Libeskind's Jewish Museum runs counter to other Berlin developments in its attempt to recognize the complexity of the city's history, rather than to simplify it.**

Despite the nostalgia of buildings like the reconstituted Hotel Adlon (left), the presence of multinational giants like Sony will make the new Berlin very different from anything it has been before. Helmut Jahn's Sony Centre on Potsdamer Platz (above).

will affect them whether they like it or not.

Take minimalism. This started as a high-minded artistic movement of the 1960s and 1970s, and was adapted by architects in the 1980s as a reaction to the superficial excesses of postmodernism. Its inspiration comes from Cistercian monasteries and Japanese houses, its objective a spiritual world of Zen simplicity. By stripping away superficial detail, it renounces the froth of the everyday. It encourages contemplation and directs attention to simple, timeless things: the grain of wood, the fall of light, the sheen of steel, the coolness of stone.

Minimalist architects were and are capable of creating beautiful spaces, but their approach was always easily reduced to a look and therefore a commodity. From the beginning there was something of Marie Antoinette's playing at milkmaids in minimalism's expensive imitations of poverty. In due course it was adopted for the flagship store of Calvin Klein, one of the most hedonistic figures in the world of fashion. Nothing wrong with that, except that it revealed minimalism for what it is: a fashion statement like any other.

The next step was for 'minimalist' to become a term denoting anything white or off-white in the interior design sections of newspapers, and for Anouska Hempel, former erotic actress, model and socialite, to create The Hempel, a luxurious hotel that opened in 1996. Hempel had previously created Blakes, an opulently decorated 'boutique' hotel, but felt that the sophisticated market in which she operates was ready for minimalism. The resulting building is pretty good, but a Cistercian monastery it isn't, nor does it have

much in common with those serious minded artists of the 1960s and 1970s. Minimalism, like postmodernism, is just another 'ism'.

The most astute contemporary architects have adopted more subtle methods, that allow them to work in the shifting ground between idealism and consumption, virginity and whoredom, ineffectual priggishness and selling out. They are finding ways to exploit the imaginative power of contemporary consumer and entertainment culture – its ability to conceive anything and realize anything, its latently surrealist ability to combine anything with anything else, its lack of respect for congruity, its power to seize the imagination – without accepting the simplification of human experience that goes with it.

These strategies link Toyo Ito, Rem Koolhaas, Herzog & de Meuron and Jean Nouvel, architects in whom a common spirit has been noticed by critics despite the very different external appearances of their buildings. Kazuyo Sejima, Foreign Office Architects (FOA), MVRDV and other alumni of the OMA office in Rotterdam can also be included. So, in his own way, can Frank Gehry. These architects seize on the inherent strangenesses of a world shaped by electronic communications, international finance and consumer culture – its weird shifts of scale, its juxtapositions of the local and the global, the physical and the immaterial, its odd misapplications of imagery – and make virtues of them. Actually strange, a shopping mall pretends to normality, and then has to manufacture spectacle to prevent its pretended normality becoming boring. Contemporary architecture looks for its

inspiration in this strangeness.

These architects share an aversion to anything that might package their work too readily into marketable commodities, even though, in order that they may practice, it clearly has to be in some sense marketable. They belong to no movement whose name ends in 'ism' and no critic has yet succeeded in inventing one for them. The work of each is recognizably theirs, and they are all players in the architectural star system, but they avoid a narrow range of signature characteristics, of preferred materials, techniques and forms.

Their buildings avoid the characteristics that would allow them to be seen purely as artistic objects. They prefer the most neutral possible shape, the box, which is so self-effacing that the viewer is forced to look elsewhere for the building's content, or limp, nondescript shapes, or shapes that defy immediate comprehension. Their plans avoid hierarchy and centrality, but are rather fields containing fluctuations of intensity. The plan is not seen, as it has been by architects from Le Corbusier to Richard Meier, as the score of an orchestrated artistic masterpiece. Structure is concealed or denied as much as it is revealed, and synthetic materials and artificial lighting have the same status as the natural. Materials commonly seen as humble, like polycarbonate, are given the same respect as marble. The usual emblems of architectural integrity are, in other words, studiously avoided. A kind of architectural emptiness is created for other qualities to fill.

The architect apparently most concerned with the harsh realities of globalized culture is Rem Koolhaas, whose writings record – with seemingly amoral pleasure – those

**John Pawson's store for Calvin Klein in New York puts a look based on monastic simplicity at the service of one of the most hedonistic figures in fashion.**

Rem Koolhaas is fascinated by the generic spaces of globalized culture, but his buildings could not be more specific. His Congrexpo in Lille is raw and strange, combining the harsh with the luxurious.

phenomena that a traditional architect might find most horrifying. He describes generic space, cities without qualities like Atlanta and Singapore, whose immense constructions appear to have almost no use for architecture as conventionally understood. He and his students have investigated the cities of the Pearl River Delta and the mechanics of retail, and are fascinated by the lack of sentiment involved.

Koolhaas's refusal to pass judgement on these phenomena has led him to be attacked for endorsing them, but there is nothing in his built work to suggest he is trying to emulate the dehumanizing qualities of generic space. His buildings could not, in fact, be more specific. His point seems rather to be that these phenomena exist, that architects ignore them at their peril, and that the job of an architect is to make what sense they can of them.

His master plan for Euralille, the development surrounding the Channel Tunnel station in Lille, was based on the conflict in scales between this city of one million, and the 'virtual city' of 40 million people who live within an hour-and-a-half's journey time. It is a meeting point of the local and, if not the global, the international. The elements of Koolhaas's brief are a shopping centre, a convention centre and office blocks, all of them generic types that usually bring with them generic space.

Koolhaas makes no attempt to 'regionalize' these buildings or to make their appearance in Lille, which is comparable to that of the Mori Tower in Shanghai, less shocking. But nor does he attempt to present them, as conventional architects and developers would, as normal. An ordinary shopping centre or convention

centre tries to smooth over its abrupt encounters with its surroundings, and between its different constituent elements. It tries to create smooth, undemanding spaces that soothe the visitor with carpet, artificial light and a steady temperature. Koolhaas's buildings in Lille are the opposite: they dramatize the differences between the parts, and the boundaries between them are left unresolved, 'to create and trigger potential'. The architecture is raw and strange, combining harsh elements with luxurious materials, and the natural with the artificial. If generic space is about suppressing difference, Euralille is about amplifying it.

Koolhaas's architecture is cinematic in that it consists of a series of events and scenes that can only be comprehended over a period of time, rather than at a single glance. This quality has culminated in his house in Bordeaux, completed in 1998, where an extraordinary range of spatial experiences and allusions are compressed into a three-storey space. In this respect his buildings have something in common with themed space, which is also cinematic in inspiration, and, like themed space, the Bordeaux house is an artificial landscape, a highly synthetic world that stands in for the natural environment. Unlike themed space, Koolhaas's architecture lacks the ambition of subordinating everything to a single, scripted experience.

The notion of landscape is a strong one among contemporary architects, including those like FOA and the Dutch practice MVRDV, whose principals worked for Koolhaas at OMA. It allows architects to think of their buildings as fields for possibly unpredictable activities rather than as finite architectural objects. It

suggests a way of exerting architectural influence which, being difficult to objectify, is difficult to turn into a mere commodity. It also appropriates a powerful technique of themed space and shopping malls, which is to envelop the consumer in a self-sufficient landscape, and turn it to different ends.

In MVRDV's VPRO building in Hilversum, the building-as-landscape notion is made explicit by the installation of a grass roof, as well as by sloping floors and the interpenetration of internal and external ground planes. As in many contemporary buildings, ground level – that absolute datum and source of stability for classical architecture – is made ambiguous. Inside, the building's several levels are designed to seem as much as possible parts of the same, continuous, folded plane, on which the building's users are encouraged to establish their own territories. This folding and intersecting is the building's primary architectural technique, a fact underlined by the uningratiating and enigmatic exterior, whose lack of obvious sense tells the viewer to look beyond the façade for the building's substance.

FOA's Yokohama International Port Terminal, where the disembarking passengers of cruise ships and ferries will encounter the public life of Yokohama, deals with a meeting of the local and the distant comparable to that at Euralille. FOA's strategy is also to create a landscape of warping, sloping, bifurcating and intersecting planes, within which the territories of passengers and locals can define themselves. The terminal is neither city nor boat, but a third space with its own highly consistent qualities. Unlike a shopping mall

**Architects such as Kazuyo Sejima are more interested in properties like transparency than architectural form. Gifu housing (left). Foreign Office Architects' Yokohama International Port Terminal seeks to create a fluid space within which different users can define their own territory (right).**

Peter Zumthor's
thermal baths at Vals
gains its power from
the environmental
and sensual properties
of its materials (above
and overleaf).

but like Euralille, its purpose is to exploit the differences, frictions and strangenesses inherent in the building's programme – in this case the meeting of transient and urban – and not to create homogenized space. In both the VPRO building and the terminal, the creation of an artificial landscape is combined with raw finishes and an openness to the exterior, both of which qualities are the antithesis of themed space.

There is a similar combination of borrowing and opposing in contemporary architects' use of sensory experience. The 'experience' is an essential feature of consumer space, whether in the form of a ride or a theme or simply shopping, and its status has been consecrated by naming Britain's celebration of the year 2000 the 'New Millennium Experience'. Like the self-sufficient landscape, it has the power to embrace the consumer's entire being.

In Kazuyo Sejima's Gifu housing, what looks at first like a standard modernist apartment block is made exceptional by its experiential qualities. The surprising thinness of the block gives it translucency and its elevations are animated by the shadows of people inside. The block is also punctured with square openings that run through its depth, which are actually terraces for individual flats. Together with the translucent walls, these make the block into a field of varying degrees of light, which on closer examination is found to relate to the way the block is inhabited.

Works like Peter Zumthor's thermal baths at Vals and Herzog & de Meuron's Dominus winery in California are environments dominated by experience. As architectural forms they are largely uninteresting, but gain all their power from the environmental, sensual properties of particular materials. In the baths at Vals, the palpable weight of its thick schist walls give the building a physical presence like that of a human body, which the material's hardness and coldness simultaneously contradicts, just as the baths' vapourous atmosphere contradicts the building's solidity. In the winery, there is light filtering through the gabion stone walls, the natural cool these stones create, and the play of the massive walls against fragile glass partitions inside.

The insistence on the intrinsic properties of (in these cases) natural materials is the opposite of themed space, where intrinsic properties are suppressed so that materials can better represent something else, and better follow their script. But this insistence is not that of a modernist or a minimalist architect, who would present a beautiful material in the plainest possible form. Instead, the viewer's perception is ambushed by paradoxes and inversions. The stones in Herzog & de Meuron's gabion walls are at once massive and levitating, load-bearing walls and roof membrane, ancient masonry and borrowings from modern road construction.

These paradoxes are one way of resisting the simplification by which something can be reduced to a commodity. They also respond to the fact that, in a world where perception is conditioned by electronic media, the image of something and its material presence are two separate things. To insist with neolithic certitude that a stone is a stone is a stone is a little naive, when it could equally well be an electronic simulation of a stone.

Herzog & de Meuron say their work reveals the strange in the ordinary, which is perhaps why they were chosen to design the new Tate Gallery of Modern Art in the former Bankside power station, a building in some senses both ordinary and strange. The new Tate is the latest in a line of grand art palaces, which function as major public spaces as well as machines for viewing art, and which, from the Pompidou Centre in Paris to the Staatsgalerie in Stuttgart, to the Louvre Pyramid, the Bilbao Guggenheim and the Getty Centre in California, form the definitive architectural landmarks of the past 25 years.

What is unusual about the new Tate is that this cultural, urban and architectural trophy should be inserted into a redundant functional building of no great historic value, the charms of whose dour brick exterior are strictly for connoisseurs. Certainly the power station's retention baffled many British commentators, who saw it as an example of conservationism gone mad, as well as many of the architects who competed to design the new Tate, whose schemes would have worked better if the power station wasn't there.

They missed the point, however. As an industrial relic in the heart of London, Bankside represents a condition typical of cities throughout the post-industrial world. Also typical is the conversion of such places into leisure or cultural use, a shift that is as strange as it is commonplace. By transforming rather than replacing this ostensibly ordinary building, the Tate is dramatizing rather than obliterating the strangenesses and contradictions of the change from industrial to cultural use. There were certain other advantages, for example artists' preferences for exhibiting in converted industrial spaces,

**As the conversion of an industrial relic, the new Tate Gallery at Bankside Power Station, London, dramatizes a condition typical of contemporary cities.**

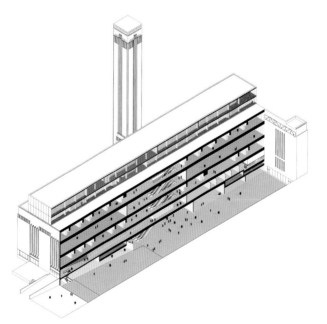

and the magnificent turbine hall of the power station, which is of a scale no architect of a new building would dare to conceive, and which is set to be one of London's great public spaces.

To have constructed a glossy new gallery would very probably have been to create a monovalent space which, like a shopping mall or a themed space, has a single, shallow, unified character that pretends to a kind of normality. What is actually under construction is something that will, with its central atrium, inward looking organization and browsing population, have some of the qualities of a mall, but will also, thanks to the retention of recalcitrant fabric from the past, allow complexity and richness. The power station's very lack of prettiness prevents it becoming merely quaint, like Covent Garden market in London or South Street Seaport in New York. The most important part of Herzog & de Meuron's job has been knowing what to leave alone and what to build anew in translating this industrial fortress into a major public building.

The same aversion to the tabula rasa can be seen in Latz and Partner's park in Duisburg, Germany, which demonstrates another common post-industrial situation; a huge former steelworks strewn with half-derelict structures, its soil contaminated. One approach would be, as has happened to make way for the Millennium Dome, to remove much of the contaminated land to another unfortunate site elsewhere, to contain the rest beneath a clay cap, and to pray. Another approach would be to venerate the old blast furnaces and sintering plants as objects of industrial heritage.

Latz and Partner are doing neither. Instead they have devised techniques that allow the land slowly to become safe, and for the population of Duisburg gradually to inhabit the park. With some deft moves – a grove of saplings supported on iron bars, a field of flowers, an area of paving made out of eight-tonne iron plates, an open-air stage – the structures are made into a series of settings for public life without losing the quality of ruins. The canals that form part of the decontamination works, and the walkways that take people safely over the areas that are still dangerous, are made into part of the fabric of the park.

A scene of destruction has been converted into an asset for the city, and a place of hopelessness into a place of pride. For better or for worse, the identity of a town like Duisburg

is tied up with its industrial past. The park honours that past, while enabling it to be converted into a source of renewed life. It is also a landscape of artificial nature, where the man-made and the natural fuse and overlap, which rings more true than would any attempt to create an image of untrammelled nature.

## Bilbao's rollercoaster

There is no position of absolute moral purity open to architects, and no guarantee of integrity or of 'good architecture'. Few buildings are unambiguously 'good' or 'bad'. The contemporary architecture that seems to ring true, which seems to be somehow most apt to the moment, is created by architects who come close to embracing the cultures of consumption and of theming, but who maintain the ability to discriminate and choose within these cultures. They are guilty neither of naive ignorance of the circumstances that surround them, nor of cynical acceptance of whatever these circumstances might press them to do. Such architects have both self-awareness and an awareness of contemporary culture outside architecture. They are sensitive to the cultural and perceptual context in which they work. This position of awareness, and of sustained moral ambiguity, accounts for the critical and popular success of the Bilbao Guggenheim, a building that exploits the power of modern entertainment culture, but not its values.

Its architect, Frank Gehry, is in some ways the ultimate signature architect, the alter-ego of Richard Meier for those who like things a bit rougher, whose instantly recognizable trademark style is eagerly bought into by

**By choosing adaptation rather than obliteration of the former Thyssen steelworks in Duisburg, Latz and Partner honour the past while creating a source of renewed life (above).**

**The Bilbao Guggenheim shows that, at a time of electronic communication, theming, shopping and generic space, sheer physical building can still have power (overleaf).**

institutions and companies. There is a lot of form-making in his buildings, a lot of gestures that say 'this is architecture' in the strongest possible terms. The Bilbao Guggenheim, as the local franchise of the New York museum, is an extension into museum building of an idea popularized by McDonald's. Many in Bilbao, a depressed industrial town whose Basque population gives it a more than usually intense local identity, felt that the museum represented cultural colonization, for which their government had to pay handsomely. Given these facts, the Guggenheim could easily have been just another trophy, another urban Rolex for a city that could ill afford it.

The building is also pure spectacle, and looks as astonishing as it could. Inside, the twisting balconies of its atrium are as much like a rollercoaster as a building can be

without actually moving. The software that shaped its impossible shapes is, as Tony Vidler has pointed out, the same as that used to simulate dinosaurs in *Jurassic Park*. It has the hallmarks of themed and retail space. A conglomeration of many parts around a central space, it has pretensions to be a city all by itself. It has abrupt transitions of scale. It is an all-embracing experience. It is, like any art gallery, like a big shop where you can't actually buy anything. It is a place you experience by browsing. Its plan has certain similarities to that of Jon Jerde's CityWalk.

All these things make it powerful, and highly accessible to an international audience that has seen a lot of films and television, and done a lot of shopping. But it is also more than that, for Gehry has exploited the strangenesses of the situation, such as the sudden

appearance of this slice of Fifth Avenue in the Basque country and the placing of a palace of art on this particular site, poised between a goods yard, some nineteenth-century apartments and a river, pierced and overflown by railways and a flyover. Such strangenesses are characteristic of contemporary life.

The Guggenheim is accordingly palatial and industrial, its shapes swirling in the eddies of surrounding transport, its tentacles hooking under the flyover. It is unafraid of using direct metaphors, most obviously that of a boat, but it doesn't push them to the point of banality. Its titanium cladding seems to belong to the shipbuilding world of the river but it also, by virtue of being an unusual material, has a certain other-worldly weirdness.

The popular success of the Guggenheim and the global attention it has attracted shows that, even at a time of electronic communications, of theming and shopping, of generic space, and of all the other phenomena that outpace, bypass and devalue sheer physical building, a work of architecture can still have power. It can also exploit a repertoire of forms, materials and techniques never previously available to architects, so that the kind of freedom once found only in modestly scaled buildings like Le Corbusier's Ronchamp can now be realized in major public buildings.

This power is not achieved by reiterating old certainties, nor by embracing uncritically the values of consumer culture, but by a certain principled fluidity, an openness to events, the ability to choose when to change and when to leave alone, an enjoyment of the contemporary world in all its complexity.

Situated just across the Thames from St Paul's, the new Tate is intended to revitalize a neglected district of London (left). Bankside Power Station, a formerly impenetrable brick fortress, is being made into the world's largest museum of modern art (right).

# The Tate Gallery of Modern Art, London Cool energy art experience

Raymund Ryan

**Smaller art spaces by Herzog & de Meuron – the Goetz Gallery in Munich and the Rémy Zaugg studio (above) – served as prototypes for the Tate Gallery. Bankside Power Station's turbine hall before conversion work started (left).**

In the early twentieth century, art and architecture fell deeply in love with the machine. From Duchamp's 'Bride Stripped Bare by her Bachelors, Even' to the urbanistic fantasies of the Russian constructivists and of Le Corbusier, the Modern Movement flourished on mass industrialization and the industrialization of the masses. That romance has long gone sour. Modernism has had to retreat.

In today's so-called developed cities, the generic environment suffers from a kind of aesthetic and economic hangover, with significant properties lying vacant and many neighbourhoods no longer possessing a clear *raison d'être*. Current art practice is marked by experiments with symbols and communication and meaning at a time when technology, and its control, is increasingly invisible.

London's new Tate Gallery of Modern Art brings together these themes of the post-industrial city and contemporary art practice in the skilful, appropriate and very public regeneration of Bankside Power Station.

### Urban realities

Bankside is one of those lonely buildings that many people regularly see but few have ever visited. Or even thought about very much. All the more intriguing then that this mountain of brick is not in some distant landscape but in the bustling heart of London. An enormous volume, free-standing and virtually opaque, Bankside rises up beside the Thames with views north to St Paul's Cathedral and the City, the disorder of Southwark to the south. The way in which Bankside appears forgotten, stranded, or anachronistic is partly

what makes it so interesting today.

In London, power and significant architecture have tended to congregate north of the Thames. The river has been both a means of communication and a barrier. As the City developed into the nation's business centre and Westminster grew into the locus of religious, political and royal pageantry, the South Bank attracted little serious design attention. Today, its ordinariness may be south London's greatest asset. The Borough of Southwark boasts a well-known Gothic cathedral but its general ambience derives from its corner shops, traffic roundabouts and autochthonous workshops that one immediately recognizes as the fabric of daily life.

The new Tate looks towards the splendour of postcard London but it is surrounded by the normality and grittiness of everyday reality. With its epic bulk and a grand, central chimney, Bankside was clearly built to generate electrical power. Like its sibling station upriver at Battersea (and the classic British telephone box), Bankside was designed by the traditionalist architect Sir Giles Gilbert Scott and built between 1947 and 1963. In twentieth-century London however, most architectural opinion, seduced by functionalism, was opposed to Scott's classical composition. But unfashionability may again have it virtues: the restraint of Scott's architecture – its timelessness – has given Bankside an unmistakable monumentality.

The electricity station is layered in zones running east–west behind the 99-metre- (325-foot-) high chimney stack, parallel with the Thames but removed some distance from it. The finished building is thus a series of boxes or parallelepipeds,

each with its programmatic specificity, with a parvis facing towards the river and a swathe of grass covering oil-storage tanks to the south. The entire exposed structure is clad in brown brick with brick vertical window dividers and banded finials that provide modest ornamentation. If Bankside has its Egyptian quality – the power station as temple of the twentieth century – these details hint at art deco.

Inside the brick carapace, Bankside's interior is a remote world of girders, rivets and gantries – a steel Valhalla. Its northern section – the boiler house – was filled through several storeys with technical equipment. But its southern half, not exactly a twin, is one single volume measuring 152 × 24 × 30 metres (1,500 × 80 × 100 feet). This was the turbine room, a great chamber undifferentiated on the exterior in which machinery ruled and workers were reduced to a minuscule scale. Here in the heart of London is a place worthy of *Metropolis* or *Modern Times*, a nave of industrial activity, a hermetic dinosaur surviving into the postmodern era.

### Tate 2000

The sugar baron Henry Tate established the National Gallery of British Art in 1897. During the ensuing decades, the museum became known by its benefactor's name but also – due to the conservative nature of other institutions – began to be the most important exhibitor of progressive international art. Hence a dichotomy in the Tate's role and purpose: on the one hand, home to British art from Elizabethan miniatures to paintings by Spencer and Freud; on the other, host to modernist and postmodernist works from Matisse

and Rothko to Nauman and Gilbert and George.

As its holdings grew, and as activities became more frequent and more varied, the Tate's premises at Millbank became inflexible. Between 1985 and 1996, the number of visitors more than doubled. During this period, the Clore Gallery was added by James Stirling and Michael Wilford as a small wing tailored to the Tate's superb Turner Collection. The Tate of the North (also by Stirling Wilford) and the Tate of the West (by Evans & Shalev) opened in Liverpool (1988) and St Ives (1993) respectively. But the fundamental problems of space and direction at Millbank remained largely unresolved. Small, sensitive additions would not suffice.

Thus the Tate finally decided to uncouple its twin agenda: to leave its British collection at Millbank (in a £30 million reorganization by John Miller) and to look elsewhere for suitable space to accommodate international art produced since 1900. The Tate could have commissioned such flamboyant new architecture as the Getty complex in Los Angeles (by Richard Meier) or the Bilbao Guggenheim (by Frank Gehry). Instead, heedful of the heterogeneity of recent art practice as well as the changing fabric of London, it decided to reuse the redundant shell of Bankside.

Immediately, Bankside's stark and unrepeatable form provides the Tate with a new symbol and its 3.4 hectares (8.5 acres) of site the possibility of a unique riverside park. The vast interior contains the sort of anonymous space favoured by contemporary artists and curators. But with its indomitable external presence and great void of the turbine hall, Bankside's galleries

**A footbridge by Foster and Partners will link the new Tate to the City. The 120-metre (400-foot) two-storey 'light beam' on the roof will be the strongest external sign of the building's conversion.**

Tate Gallery of Modern Art

Sculpture Display

Exhibition Galleries

Collection Displays

Bankside

Concourse

Level 3

Information

Exhibi

Tate Shop

Tate Shop

The immense turbine hall (above) will become a public space (left). Some of the new galleries (top), with clerestory lighting, are similar to the spaces within the Goetz Gallery.

could never be completely neutral. The most exciting aspect of the new Tate is this tension between scales and textures, context and contents, physical bulk and the unpredictable nature of future events.

Although renovation of post-industrial space has become standard for commercial galleries and smaller museums, no institution for contemporary art has yet tried reuse at this scale – 11,148 square metres (120,000 square feet) of exhibition space – and degree of prestige. London's Saatchi and Los Angeles's Temporary Contemporary galleries are smaller. In general, reuse offers advantages of cost, flexibility, ambience and the absence of academic or authoritative relationships that postmodernism claims to undermine.

Deliberately, the Tate's efforts and the associated public funds are being distributed about the capital. Some distance from Millbank, Southwark is an area in obvious need of a large catalytic project. With a total budget estimated at £130 million, £50 million has already been allocated to the Bankside project by the Millennium Commission via the National Lottery and a further £12 million by English Partnerships, the government's Urban Regeneration Agency. When the Gallery opens in the year 2000, it is expected to create over 2,000 new jobs, mostly in the immediate vicinity.

To choose an architect, the Tate set up symposia on the nature of contemporary museums. Then, in an ambitious two-stage competition (comparable only to that for New York's MoMA two years later), an initial list of 148 architectural practices was reduced first to thirteen and then to six. The final six firms – all of which produced

detailed drawings and models – were those of Tadao Ando (Japan), David Chipperfield (England), Rafael Moneo (Spain), Rem Koolhaas/Richard Gluckman (the Netherlands), Renzo Piano (Italy), and the eventual winners, Jacques Herzog and Pierre de Meuron from Basel in Switzerland.

### (almost) No design

The winners wisely allow Bankside to stand as it is. Scott's building will not be obscured or needlessly altered by architectural gamesmanship. It's a question of modification. The Herzog & de Meuron proposal is literally marked by two subservient moves: the addition of a luminous penthouse across the entire run of the riverside frontage and the excavation of the turbine hall to create an inner public space accessible by ramp. The ground surface is freed for public use.

Whereas the double-storey penthouse sits on top of Bankside as an inhabited billboard scaled to the metropolitan condition, the broad ramp to the turbine hall has a more local significance. It begins the formal entry sequence out in the park as a bold earthwork informing the neighbourhood. If the penthouse is about lightness and addition, the ramped entry hall is about weight and subtraction.

Bankside's north parvis is thought of as a hard, urban place, a grand terrace animated by pedestrians and joggers along the riverside path. The parvis will be linked directly to the City by a second millennium project, a footbridge designed (by the architect Sir Norman Foster and sculptor Sir Anthony Caro) to align with Wren's dome at St Paul's. To

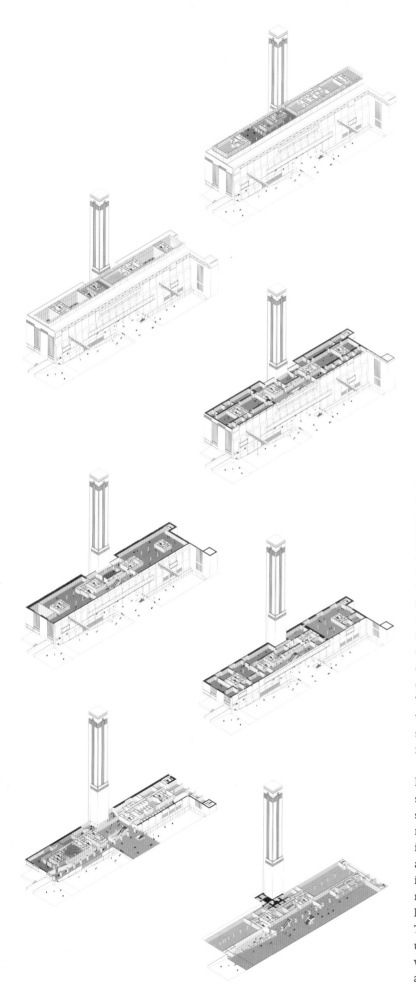

benefit from this picturesque scene, it is planned to lease Bankside's chimney stack as a spectacular viewing tower.

Designed in conjunction with the Zurich-based landscape firm of Kienast Vogt, the gardens and sculpture courts surrounding Bankside proper will function round-the-clock. There will be neither gates nor fences. With entrances at all four cardinal points, the gallery will thus stand upon a new kind of inside/outside, barrier-free surface, an inviting and welcome improvement for this part of London.

The entry ramp descends into the bowels of the turbine hall to flow beneath an open viewing platform with the old gantries still in place far above. It's a tourist ha-ha, acting as a discrete mechanism for the dispersal of visitors. Aligned with the chimney, the transverse deck crosses the hall's longitudinal axis as a continuation of the riverfront terrace. It becomes an obvious gathering point – a raised crossroad – in the soaring space conceived as a grand public arcade. The galleries are entered beneath the deck, with a direct stair to supplement the ramp as primary means of access.

South of the turbine hall, a third layer of building contains an extant still-humming London Electricity sub-station. Although not to be renovated in time for the gallery's inauguration in the year 2000, the architects envisage this strip as an important filter of shops and neighbourhood cafés. Beyond this layer, on the Southwark side, the Tate also hopes to develop several underground storage tanks as a venue for the latest art installations and happenings. As yet

aspirational, these subsidiary display volumes would greatly augment the relationship between Bankside and its hinterland.

To date, the work of Herzog & de Meuron has been noteworthy for the extraordinary qualities it has achieved in often quite ordinary circumstances. Their feeling for the everyday manifests itself in the factories and sports halls and apartment buildings built in the periphery of Basel, part and parcel of contemporary urban life. For these designers, architecture and urbanism are inextricable activities. Of course, the practice does not just replicate the ordinary. By revealing certain inherent qualities, often through juxtaposition or superimposition, their work achieves paradoxical effect. Herzog & de Meuron's proposal for Bankside almost disappears into its urban fabric. It will only be understood *in situ*, through physical and sensory experience.

### Let there be light

The design is almost no design at all. Its principal generator is perception and light. This engagement with light is more than mere professional practicality. Both architects have long been associated with artists and spaces in which to view art. In the early 1990s, they built the small Goetz gallery in Munich with a thick band of birch appearing to hover between a dado and a cornice of translucent glass. Their work with Joseph Beuys (for the 1978 Basel carnival) and their collaborations with artists such as Helmut Federle, Rémy Zaugg and Thomas Ruff, has had a direct role in the way their buildings exhibit themselves.

Cutaway axonometric showing the ramped entrance to the turbine hall and the internal elevation of the gallery floors (below). Axonometrics showing the gallery's seven main levels (left).

The elevation of the gallery floors on to the turbine hall. The intention is to make the internal arrangement of the galleries comprehensive from the hall. The long horizontal windows, set against the black wall, will echo the 'light beam' on the building's roof (overleaf).

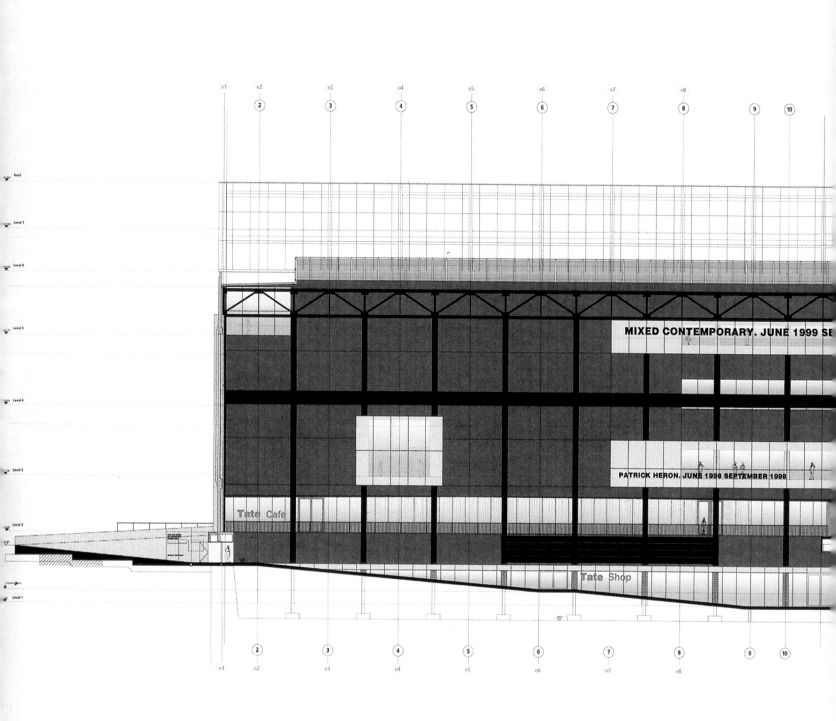

MIXED CONTEMPORARY. JUNE 1999 SE

PATRICK HERON. JUNE 1998 SEPTEMBER 1998

Tate Cafe

Tate Shop

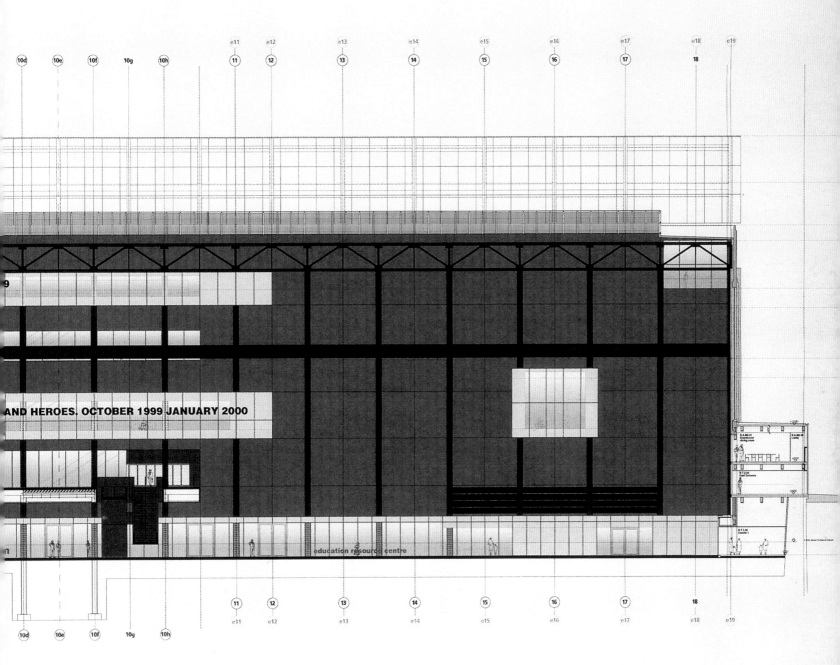

AND HEROES. OCTOBER 1999 JANUARY 2000

education resource centre

At Bankside, light is manipulated not only for the display of art but also to organize the visitor's comprehension of the institution. Entering the turbine hall, visitors will experience an unprecedented space lit from above and inhabited with large-scale sculptures and installations. Through an enormous inserted screen, they will see into the cafeteria and lower-level bookstore. Linear light-boxes will project from the galleries stacked above to serve as signage screens and to connect new exhibition floors within the boiler house with the vertiginous chasm of the turbine hall. These vitrines reappear on the north face as the cafeteria pushes through from under the monumental cliff of bricks to view the riverside.

At ground level, the cafeteria, the cinema/lecture theatre and various administrative offices are independent of the core gallery circuit. Visitors descend to the excavated floor of the turbine hall and then ascend rapidly via glass-encased escalators – bypassing the ground level – to three floors of galleries. These break into wings either side of the central chimney with its new 'picture windows' on to the river. These wings then subdivide into core and satellite chambers where the absence of obtrusive fittings or decoration helps achieve a vital calm. An open, ceremonial stairway runs through all three galleries.

The creation of these subsidiary and somewhat sequential volumes will allow the Tate to both deal efficiently with large crowds and to create a more intimate atmosphere before the exhibited works of art. On the lower gallery floors, light will penetrate in from the existing vertical openings in the north, east and west façades, and from the pristine light-boxes overlooking the turbine hall. There will be views out from the galleries, connecting the visitor with the surrounding city.

Across the galleries' contiguous ceilings, lighting fixtures will be recessed into flush, geometrically arrayed slots. The outer galleries above have identical slots but use direct daylight, thus forming a matrix of illumination that virtually perforates the entire building. Beneath the penthouse, the topmost galleries are lit by twin strips of clerestory window. It promises to be a remarkable finale, with light suffusing the gap between old and new.

The Bankside penthouse is emblematic of the spirit of illumination and spatial flow throughout the new Tate. The penthouse is not homogeneous, but rather a complex hybrid. It is divided into public space (the sky restaurant) and technical equipment: a similar but non-uniform condition, vitreous and electric above the dark 'industrial era' carcass of the power station.

In this most provocative yet indigenous of settings, London will finally be able to host major international exhibitions. Herzog & de Meuron have harnessed the Tate's technical obligations to art with a desire to be in the public realm. Their proposal neither annihilates the past nor predetermines the future, but resuscitates the former and presents options for the latter. The distinct paradox of Bankside is that a heavy and intimidating structure is made delicate and inviting. After the dogma of modernism, Bankside makes architecture look easy.

At the Reichstag (left) and Potsdamer Platz (facing page), Berlin is acquiring a new political and civic identity.

# Berlin 1999
# Phantoms and formulae

Brian Hatton

In Berlin just now they're beginning again; but in Berlin, new beginnings are nothing new. 1287: Seat of Mark Brandenburg; eighteenth century: Kingdom of Prussia; 1871: Kaiser-capital; 1919: Republican metropolis; 1933: Third Reich *Machtstadt*; 1945: Communist bastion. Now, they are rebeginning it as *Bundeshauptstadt*, or 'Federal Chief City' of the most successful, prosperous democracy Germany has known. If *Hauptstadt* translates as 'chief city', it is because, despite the huge effort being put into this new beginning, the title 'capital' is a dubious one, for reasons historical, geographical and political. For some, Prussian arrogance and Nazi tyranny have cast too many shadows to be banished, despite Berlin's traditions of enlightenment. A practical limit to its status as capital is that German commerce and industry have so spread around the Federal Republic that Berlin will not win the overbearing dominance of, for instance, London. Germany has avoided the chronic regional disparities that London's monopoly has produced in Britain; but as the former East areas were absorbed into the Federal Republic, it was seen that, if investment was not directed eastwards, Germany would develop an east-west gap as bad as Britain's north-south divide. Nevertheless, with the federal *Länder* system, and so many headquarters remaining in the west, such as the Bundesbank in Frankfurt, government relocation will not of itself generate another London or Paris.

But do the Germans want or need such a capital? Who needs capitals at all? Was not Germany always a regionalized culture, and

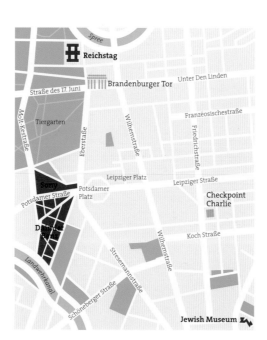

**The rebuilding of Potsdamer Platz on the wasteland where the Berlin Wall once stood is the centrepiece of Berlin's reconstruction.**

wasn't Bonn quite enough for the success of the Federal Republic? These questions were raised before the decision to move the government to Berlin. Once taken, however, the decision produced more questions about the representation and symbolism of the Republic. And all this stands before an irony, at the place where the future is to meet the past, on the site of the new capital. For are we not about to see the end in Europe (many would say 'about time, too'), of nation states and capital cities?

For over five years, Berlin has been the biggest building site in Europe, with over 700 cranes across its skyline. In the old East, there's vast refurbishing of prefabricated housing estates, new tram and underground lines, water and cable systems, and systematic upgrading of every facility from schools to luxury hotels. In the Mitte, or centre, which was also in the East, entire districts have been refitted and gentrified for new money, and the famous Friedrichstrasse has

been made over into a big-business avenue, with its own Galeries Lafayette (by Jean Nouvel) and Philip Johnson Building for US trade at the former Checkpoint Charlie. The Hamburg–Leipzig TGV will cross the Paris–Moscow line at Lehrter Bahnhof, a vast interchange near the new government centre, where dozens of new embassies are being opened. The museum systems are being reintegrated with major new galleries. Yet even amid so much rebuilding, there are strategic sites still to be resolved. Alexanderplatz, locus of Alfred Döblin's 1920s novel, and once the centre of proletarian Berlin, has yet to receive its new plan, despite a recent competition with a dazzling entry from Daniel Libeskind. At the core of old imperial Berlin, the site of the Royal Palace and the Communist Palast der Republik continues to generate heated political debate; where war had blasted so much, every monument and historical site is disputed all over again; not with bullets, but

with words and Deutschmarks.[1]

In this clamour, three sites stand out for their historic importance and new architectural representation. They are signal for the future, corresponding to the three categories – historical, economic and political – which will qualify Berlin's late identity as 'capital city'. These are the Jewish Wing of the Berlin City Museum; the rebuilt Potsdamer Platz; and the conversion of the old Reichstag to the new Bundestag.

The Jewish Museum is considered here first, because it relates to the past in two important ways. It is the only one of the three projects to have been conceived before the fall of the Wall, and its theme is the historical fate of Germany's and Berlin's greatest minority; a fate so tragic that Germany cannot proceed into the future without acknowledgment and expiation. Since 1945, various attempts have been made to give expression to this process, by preservation of extermination camps, educational programmes, and, across the country, Holocaust memorials. Yet, as the current Berlin debate and recent Vienna debacle show, the 'memorial problem' proves all but unsolvable: how can a monument speak the exorbitant, untellable horror of mass-murder?

Increasingly, it is generally conceded that the most successful of the 'public signs' to mark the Nazi barbarity have been those that replaced the traditional stamp of the 'monument' with silent withdrawal. An example is the cryptic but moving symbol erected in the university square to mark the eclipse of intellectual freedom, on the spot where the Nazis rehearsed their burning of bodies by the

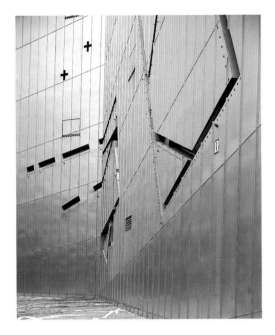

The Jewish Museum is an extension to the Berlin Museum, which is housed in a baroque palace (overleaf, left). Libeskind employs dramatically contrasting architecture, but the two buildings are connected underground, and the complex as a whole is intended to demonstrate how, before the Nazis, Berlin life and Jewish life were inextricably linked.

In Daniel Libeskind's Jewish Museum, the 'Garden of Exile' (right) represents Berlin Jews' experiences of forced exile. The plan, derived from a fragmented Star of David, is penetrated by the long, straight Holocaust Void, representing the violent interruption of Berlin Jewish life (below, right).

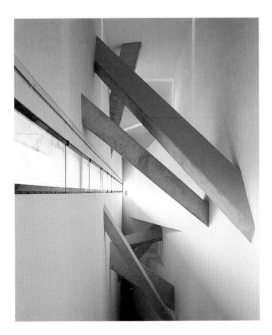

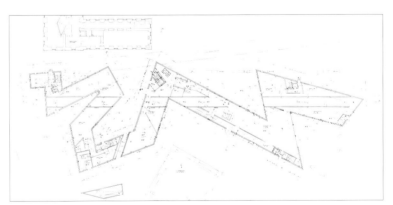

The redevelopment of
Potsdamer Platz is led
by major corporations.
The Sony Centre, by
Helmut Jahn (below)
and the Debis Building
by Renzo Piano
(facing page).

The Cinemaxx Centre
by Ulrike Lauber and
Wolfram Wöhr (left).

burning of books: a window set into the ground looking down into an empty library.[2]

More comprehensive account of the intrinsic part of Jewry in Berlin culture and community has been slower coming. From the rubble of 'Year Zero', 1945, the City Museum had been gradually curated in the baroque Kollegienhaus, one of the few survivors (just) of the formally laid-out eighteenth-century district of Friedrichstadt. Only in 1989 was a competition held to find a design for an extension of the City Museum to display its collection of Judaica previously split between the Kollegienhaus and Martin Gropius Bau. Now the aim was to assemble it all, showing the special contribution of Jews to the history and life of Berlin in a new wing of signal distinction.

In traditional procedure, curators collect, preserve and display things, and their display sets an agenda or brief for the architect. But recently, cultural institutions have become such civic icons that their public form is their prime architectural driver. The Jewish Wing was bound even more to a symbolic demand. More than just a collection, it assumed the salience of a monument. Yet it fell into the dilemma of other such markers; the more so because it was no bare 'Holocaust memorial' but had the task of showing the continuity and rupture between Jewry and Berlin. Monument/ antimonument, continuity/ rupture: a brief of contraries.

Daniel Libeskind, the designer of the museum, came to prominence in Berlin two years earlier with his 'City Edge' project for Friedrichstadt's fringe, where the district's orderly grid of avenues and

once-regulated blocks frayed into a wilderness of old marshalling yards. The project was part of the International Building Exhibition (IBA) a programme, mostly of housing, evolved over 15 years to rebind the blighted districts along the Wall. There were two agendas: 'old-build', areas of community refurbishment with the slogan 'careful urban renewal', and 'new-build', where the concept of 'critical reconstruction' guided the design of dozens of projects in Tiergarten and Friedrichstadt. What in fact was being 'critically reconstructed' was not the substance but a certain idea of the city; an idea largely modelled on the baroque formalism of the Friedrichstadt plan, with its discipline of roofline, streetline and typical courtyard, or *Hinterhof*. Yet Josef-Paul Kleihues, the 'new-build' coordinator, saw that conformity would not suit certain sites, as well as being inappropriate for some of the designers IBA had recruited, such as Rem Koolhaas, and others who later became associated with 'deconstruction', such as Eisenman, Hadid and Libeskind.[3]

'City Edge' was like no other IBA project. A 'train crash' of oblique slabs and jagged shards, it was everything that Kleihues' Friedrichstadt was not; it simultaneously questioned both rationalism and contextualism. What, after all, could 'contextual politeness' mean in a place where industrialism had replaced classicism, civilization had been dispatched in cattlewagons and bombs had blown apart everything? What sort of rationality prevails by ruling out in advance as 'other' any trace of unpleasantness it cannot comprehend? Jacques Derrida has pointed out that this

The Potsdamer Platz
development viewed
from the InfoBox, the
temporary building
erected to inform
the public of new
developments
(previous page).

binary division into essence and other is a basic metaphysical manoeuvre of Western rationalism, its abused form underwriting innumerable proscriptions, exclusions and exterminations. The work of philosophy is to rethink this from within rationality, alert to its slippage and ruses, respacing them, as it were, in reflexive manoeuvres. Statements of a form 'architecture is...' and 'order is...' are to be countered with 'what if...' and 'why not?' as a test to architecture from within.

Berlin's tendencies to normative order have periodically provoked discontents, such as the Expressionists of 1912, or the organic manifestos of Hans Scharoun's Culture Forum, the Philharmonie Concert Hall and State Library. But deconstruction is not expressionism: the former proceeds through its own logic of exposed contraries to 'reinscribe' 'alterity'. The Jew, it was seen, was both intrinsic to Berlin and made 'other'; the new wing was part of, yet distinct from, the rest of the museum; it was not a monument yet was bound to affirm. Libeskind's idea was to make a kind of open occultation, 'Between the Lines' as he called it, from procedures that might be criticized on a more prosaic building as mystifying acrostics; but this was no normal project. Having chosen Libeskind for precisely his poetic facility, clients and public were bound to follow the allusive lines that he now traced. Until finished, therefore, it is impossible to evaluate this building without retracing Libeskind's allegory. From addresses of notable Jewish and gentile Berlin writers, composers and artists, Libeskind anamorphically projected a Star of David across the site by the Kollegienhaus. From Walter Benjamin's *One Way Street*, he cast another 'line of leaving' across the Star, and from a score of references (the list of Berlin's deported and murdered Jews, the poet Paul Celan, Schoenberg's unfinished opera *Moses and Aaron* and uncanny storyteller ETA Hofmann, who worked in the Kollegienhaus), Libeskind wove an 'irrational matrix' to recast the Star into a wing of Klee's and Benjamin's 'Angelus Novus', a lightning-bolt, a dragon, an irruption. Through it, the 'line of leaving' left a trail of negations, absences and voids.[4]

Can a symbol be new-invented by a single poet, or may it only evolve through a culture? This question always faces the collective art of architecture. Internally, the wing's allegoric form must accommodate curatorial programmes. Externally, it cannot decline a dialectic with the city, whether it presents itself as a model for imitation or as a visionary singularity. Subsequent developments in Berlin have hardened this dialectic antagonistically. Under Hans Stimmann, Berlin's Building Senate (*Bausenat*) required that new buildings conform to what many felt was a reductive parody of IBA guidelines on block-form and stone-finish. Resistance to this coercion, led by Libeskind, has been widespread.[5]

Yet if Libeskind's design creatively deploys deconstructive ruses to deny facile or reductive reading and reach an allusive equal to Berlin's disrupted history, there is one 'metaphysic of presence' or 'closure' that it does not deconstruct: that of the authored object, or authored interpretation – which is what 'allegory' amounts to here. Planning rule and poetic rebus alike refer interpretation to authority; the architectural place where both are exceeded by the real is not the individual building but the city. As Libeskind's allegory and the post-IBA ordinances began to emerge, Berlin was transformed by the epochal events of autumn 1989. The fall of the Wall suddenly amplified its debates from marginal to momentous and its design to a matter of national destiny. But like Kafka's *A Crossbreed*, half cat, half sheep, this heirloom was an ambiguous hybrid: 'A little boy once received as his inheritance a cat, and through it became Mayor of London. What shall I become through my creature? Where stretches the gigantic city?'[6]

The site where this hybrid's rupture was most mangled, where the vanity of design most exposed was Potsdamer Platz. Or rather, what once was Potsdamer Platz. In Wim Wenders' film *Wings Of Desire*, an old poet wanders the wasteland it had become, and, where the Wall cut across it, recalls it as a 1920s carousel of theatres, shops and cafés – not designed, but an effusion of common vitality – all vanished. The Wall left behind a swathe through the city like a river of sand, which some felt should become a memorial park. Yet if the hybrid city was to unify itself, here was the place where East and West must join. But how? An open exhibition of ideas was held at the Esplanade ballroom, one of only two buildings still there. Every nostrum from zero to utopia was aired; but too late: the entire site was sold within weeks to Daimler-Benz (D-B): Potsdamer Platz soon became dubbed 'Potsdaimler Platz'.[7]

The concern that a monopoly owner of such a potent locus of old Berlin life could never do it justice was expressed in an interview with Mayor Momper by the documentary film-maker Max Ophuls on the Esplanade roof overlooking the site: 'D-B are just carmakers; what do they know of how to make cities? Can they make it so that on spring mornings I could sit at a pavement table and watch the girls go by?'[8] Of course, Momper had no answer. Nobody knew if the area's teeming vivacity could be remade by investors' fiat. It had consisted of two distinct plazas, joined like the new Berlin itself into a hybrid junction: Leipziger Platz, an octagon within Friedrichstadt's formal plan, with Potsdamer Platz exploding radially at its gate. In 1991 Kleihues wrote 'Now there is an opportunity of reconstructing the historical plan of Leipziger Platz and at the same time revitalizing Potsdamer Platz – not as a hub of communications but as a magnificent urban space corresponding to the famous octagon of the Leipziger Platz.'[9] The *Bausenat*'s competition for the area was won by an IBA-like project with conforming block-lines by Hilmer + Sattler. At the same time, however, D-B had commissioned a plan by Richard Rogers, who seized on the radial site and the investors' ambitions to project a more dynamic vision of a Times Square for Berlin. In addition to 'reconstructivists' and 'deconstructivists', there were now calls to revive the 1920s fantasy of 'Chicago on the Spree'. For a 1991 exhibition, 'Berlin Tomorrow', Hans Kollhoff wrote 'Let us draw the city limits tight and stop anyone who

**Daimler-Benz Headquarters**
Architects: Renzo Piano and Christoph Kohlbecker

**Musical Theatre**
Architects: Renzo Piano and Christoph Kohlbecker

**Casino**
Architects: Renzo Piano and Christoph Kohlbecker

**Offices**
Architect: José Rafael Moneo

**Sony Headquarters**
Architects: Murphy/Jahn

**Imax Theatre**
Architects: Renzo Piano and Christoph Kohlbecker

**Hotel Grand Hyatt**
Architect: José Rafael Moneo

**Housing**
Architects: Ulrika Lauber and Wolfran Wöhr

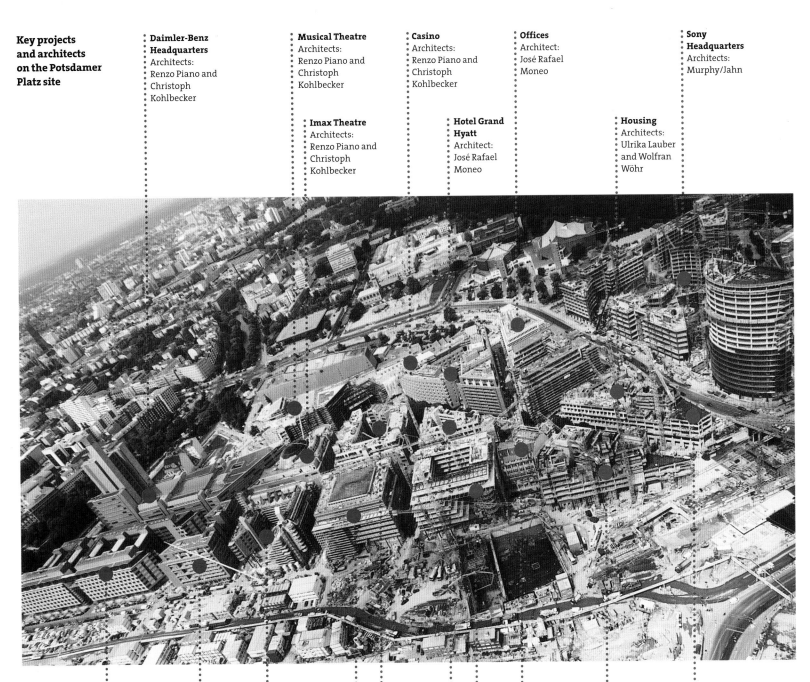

**Housing**
Architects: Renzo Piano and Christoph Kohlbecker

**Housing**
Architects: Renzo Piano and Christoph Kohlbecker

**Offices**
Architects: Renzo Piano and Christoph Kohlbecker

**Offices**
Architect: Arata Isozaki

**Housing**
Architects: Ulrika Lauber and Wolfran Wöhr

**Offices**
Architect: Richard Rogers

**Offices**
Architect: Richard Rogers

**Offices**
Architect: Hans Kollhoff

**Housing**
Architect: Richard Rogers

**Housing**
Architects: Renzo Piano and Christoph Kohlbecker

wants to relegate anything too bulky to the outskirts. Unless cosy provinciality is accepted, this cannot be achieved without American skyscrapers. Clinging to regulation height means preventing skyscrapers from releasing their urban power.'[10]

Commercial interests now drove up the pressure. Brown Boveri bought a tract of the former Potsdamer Bahnhof and Sony acquired a wedge including the Esplanade. As Rogers' plan contravened the Bausenat's block-lines and did not anticipate the railway, D-B held another competition. Renzo Piano's winning scheme balanced conflicting demands. Brown Boveri's eastern site, flanking Friedrichstadt and a park where the Bahnhof had been, would be laid out formally, initially to a plan by the neo-rationalist Georgio Grassi. The central area, west of the park, comprised a range of high-rise offices by Isozaki, Rogers, Hilmer + Sattler, Moneo and Kollhoff on a grid converging and heightening towards Potsdamer Platz. The western flank, facing the crystalline mountain of Scharoun's State Library, Piano mediated with a lake, branching from the Landwehr canal to reflect the library on one side and Piano's new skyscraper on the other. Sony's wedge went to Chicago architect Helmut Jahn, who retained the Esplanade (but moved!) within an American-style glazed atrium that recalls (in consumerist guise) the glass dreams of Berlin expressionism. This would be the side of entertainments, comprising a theatre, casino, cinemas and cafés, beside a new, sunken train station!

The consequence has been one of the biggest building sites in the world, so big that it has become a tourist attraction in itself, with an exhibition in the rather stylish 'InfoBox', constructed to orient visitors and explain to Berliners their city's future (they can even get married there). Though the scale of corporate property development may not admit the old diversity, Max Ophuls' spring-morning dream of pavement lyricism might still find its chance once the theatre of life replaces the drama of construction, when the cranes are gone and the trains arrive. It is, though, only a slender chance; mixed-use and monopoly ownership are not likely partners. Over to the east at Alexanderplatz, an exciting scheme by Libeskind to apply deconstructive tactics at urban scale would have created the kind of cultural kaleidoscope that is meant by 'metropolis' had it not fallen fallow.

If visitors look north from the InfoBox, they see another nest of cranes and a quite different kind of architectural problem: the Reichstag. The motor of Berlin's upheaval has been government; but where and how is it to be housed? But for a Luftwaffe ministry and Axis embassies, the old government quarters in Mitte and Tiergarten were obliterated. New ministries and chancellery were thus clearly indicated. But the house of parliament, the Bundestag, presented a problem because of the survival of the Kaiser's parliament, the Reichstag. On one hand, it was the obvious location historically, having been the seat also of the 1919–33 Republic. On the other, many felt that its history was too negative: it had not been a properly empowered assembly under the Kaiser; in the 1920s it never won full

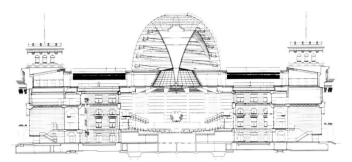

popular legitimacy and its divisions weakened democracy. Following the arson of 1933 it had been dissolved by the Nazis and became their final fortress in 1945 against the Red Army. Moreover, though finely refurbished in the 1960s by Paul Baumgarten, its interior needed to be rebuilt to house the Federal Assembly. It just didn't look right for democracy; in contrast to Günter Behnisch's recently completed Bonn Bundestag, it was opaque and heavily monumental.

Continuity won. The Reichstag was chosen and Axel Schultes' master plan was accepted for a band of ministries and democratic fora to range alongside. In autumn 1993, Sir Norman Foster was appointed to rebuild the Reichstag. His main design problem was to accommodate all the functions of a modern parliament, including the media, lobbyists and visitors. These bore typological comparison to a theatre, divided between front-of-house and backstage. Transparency, interior vistas and public access were important as well as convenience, diplomatic facility and security. At Bonn, Behnisch used armour glass to reveal the chamber; with like purpose, Foster inserted a glass wall between the chamber and west lobby, to let visitors see in immediately, as well as those following debates from the public gallery.

An intriguing question about political 'theatre' is: who designs the stage? By which we mean the arrangement of the chamber itself: who sits where? From which positions are speeches made, questions allowed, voices raised? In the orchestra, dispositions of strings, wind and percussion have evolved, but political traditions vary. The English House of Commons, a cross between church and law court, notoriously promotes adversarial debate. Republican tradition, hailing from the Greek theatre, disposes the left–right spectrum around the fan of an arc. This was the model adopted at Bonn and brought to Berlin. Among its spatial consequences is that it convokes above it the compass of a dome. The design of a dome was Foster's second, and more salient task. It did not prove straightforward.

The original 1894 design had been topped by a glass and iron canopy. This had long gone, but it was felt that some surmounting symbol would be necessary to signal the transformation of the dead Reichstag into the new Bundestag. That was why Christo's 'wrapping' of the hulk in July 1995 was so powerful. Rebuilding began the day after the unwrapping. Initially, Foster conceived a broad baldachin over its entirety with gatherings on the field before it. Eventually, concentration focused on a dome above the chamber that would let daylight down on to debates and be visible from afar. This entailed a series of elaborate models to work out the best combination of filters and reflectors to ensure even, yet altering, light around the assembly, letting fall serendipitous shafts and beams on to individual speakers.

But what is most remarkable in the final design is the way that the dome meshes with the internal programme and culminates in another symbolic device. As Baumgarten's interiors were removed (but for one room) and the fabric laid bare, it was realized that what was also being revealed was history: signs from the Kaiser, Weimar and Nazi periods were exposed, along with graffiti scribbled by exultant Russian soldiers. The visitors' circulation programme began to take on the character of an epic narrative in which democracy's vicissitudes and eclipse were followed by eventual triumph. They would move up through the public lobbies to a rooftop gallery around the lantern from which a double helix ramp would rise into the glass dome itself, displaying a historical exhibition of German democracy and the Bundestag. Down below, they would see glimpses of their representatives in argument; while above and around them would span, as Wenders' *Wings Of Desire* is named in German, 'The Skies Over Berlin'.

Foster's dome and Libeskind's labyrinth bracket the new Berlin. One offers a continuous helical assent into a lens of daylight and mastery, the other begins in descent and climbs through a zigzag into which day breaks only with the spasmodic shock of lightning and where the only whole given to the gaze is an inner yard (*Hof*), a hole sunk, it seems, as the negative shaft of hope (*Hoffnung*). Between these rarified phantoms, the mass of ordinary lives will be lived in Berlin, a *Mischlingstadt* (or 'crossbreed town'), as elsewhere. And where most will meet and mix will be a place much like Potsdamer Platz, though no one knows its formula. This was what Kracauer meant when he wrote before the war of what he called his 'unaffected Berlin' which, like a landscape, 'unconsciously holds its own'. 'Wherever massed stone meets fleeting streets, their elements arising from very different interests, random creations ensue, which are accountable to no one.'[11]

**Notes**
1. See *Lotus* 80: 'Berlin The Capital'; *Journal of Architecture* Vol. 2, No. 3: 'Berlin Eight Years On'; *Assemblage* 29; *Bauwelt* Berlin Annual 1997; 'Capitalised Assets', *Building Design*, 7.8.97.
2. On controversies over the Berlin Holocaust memorial (for which Richard Serra and Peter Eisenman have been named designers) see 'The Politics Of Memory', J. Kramer, *New Yorker*, 14.8.95, and 'Haunted Still', D. Staunton, the *Guardian*, 12.08.98. On the Vienna memorial: *Judenplatz Wien 1996*, Wien Kunsthalle & Folio Verlag, and 'Judenplatz Vienna', B. Hatton, *AA Files* 33.
3. IBA produced extensive publications; the definitive guide was its *Projektübersicht*, eds J. Kleihues & H.-W. Hämer, 1987. Also *International Building Exhibition*, J. Kleihues & H.Klotz, Academy 1987. Also 'Mending the Broken City: Interview with Kleihues', B. Hatton, *Blueprint* 54, 1989.
4. *Extension to the Berlin Museum with Jewish Department* ed. K. Feireiss is the principal introduction, with essays by K. Forster and others, and Libeskind's key text *Between the Lines*, Ernst & Sohn, 1992. ('Between the Lines' is also Libeskind's name for the project.)
5. The theoretical advocate of the 'normative' line was not Stimmann but Vittorio Lampugnani. The Libeskind-Lampugnani exchanges were reprinted in *Journal of Architecture* Vol. 1, No. 4. *cf. Lotus* 80 *op. cit.*, including 'The New Gründerzeit' by Stimmann. Also, the 1994 Architectural Design Royal Academy Symposium, later published by AD, edited by Alan Balfour.
6. In *Description Of A Struggle & Other Stories*, Franz Kafka, Penguin 1979.
7. Daimler-Benz's appropriation of the Platz was the motive of Hans Haacke's critical installation there for the 1990 exhibition 'Die Endlichkeit der Freiheit'. Haacke put D-B logos atop former guard towers at the Platz, with slogans '*Bereit sein ist alles*' (or, Readiness is All – the Wall guard motto), and '*Kunst bleibt Kunst*' (Art stays Art), Goethe's phrase, used by D-B on its arts sponsorship advertising. On Potsdamer Platz, see *The Politics Of Order*, A. Balfour, Rizzoli 1990. Also *Berlin-New York*, eds J. Kleihues & C. Rathgeber, Rizzoli 1993. In a BBC Television series, 'Building Sights', Libeskind described the Platz as 'an exemplary place in the late-twentieth century, defining what is important about architecture, cities and human life, an image of what a contemporary human being is about... with a conscious and an unconscious...'
8. In the second of two films Ophuls made on Berlin, 1989–90, Channel 4 Television.
9. 'Innovative Urban Models Need Masterplans', *AD Profile* No.92. From *Berlin Morgen*, German Architecture Museum, Frankfurt 1990.
10. See note 9 *cf.* Kollhoff in *Lotus* 80, *op. cit.*
11. In *Building Sights*, Libeskind echoed Kracauer: 'Potsdamer Platz is now both close and remote, therefore a sacred place; a place of antagonism and divisiveness. It resists interpretation and nostalgia; it brings to focus that history is unaccountable and that it surpasses architecture.'

Foster and Partners' passenger terminal is the centrepiece of Hong Kong's new airport, built on artificially formed land (right).

# Hong Kong: Chek Lap Kok The airport as saviour of the city

Martin Pawley

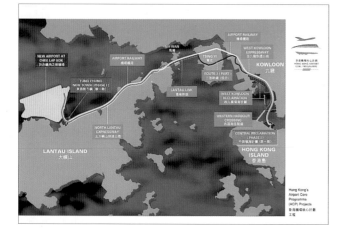

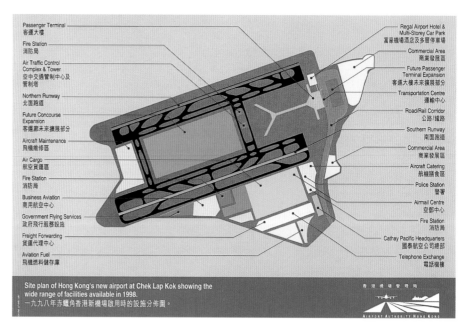

Site plan of Hong Kong's new airport at Chek Lap Kok showing the wide range of facilities available in 1998.
一九九八年赤鱲角香港新機場啟用時的設施分佈圖。

**The passenger terminal is only part of a huge infrastructural programme that includes road and rail links to Hong Kong** (left), a cargo terminal, business centre and a new town. Impression of the new airport in the year 2000 (top).

It was no accident that in July 1998, United States President Bill Clinton; People's Republic of China President Jiang Zemin; Hong Kong Special Administrative Region Chief Executive Tung Chee-hwa and hundreds of leaders, politicians, administrators and dignitaries visited the city's great new airport at Chek Lap Kok. Their presence showed that the christening of this great feat of design and construction possessed a political and economic significance not only reaching beyond the confines of the city, but beyond the urban region of the Pearl River Delta to affect all the countries of the Pacific Rim. The impact of Chek Lap Kok will continue to be felt in the battle for supremacy among the great cities of East Asia throughout the twenty-first century.

On a clear day, airline passengers circling above the islands of the Pearl River Delta look down upon an urban civilization without parallel on earth. At its centre, Hong Kong Island shoots forth high-rise towers that fit together as tightly as cigarettes in a packet; elsewhere, mountainous hinterlands are strewn with evidence of massive earth movement, landfill and construction. The built-up coastal strip either side of Hong Kong harbour is not the city's most obvious topographical feature. That title falls to the great cuts and scars in the landscape that are everywhere evidence of a vast reshaping process that will probably go on for as long as Hong Kong survives as a great city.

'Slope control', as this cutting and stabilizing process is called, is part of the work of tunnelling, bridging, road building and land reclamation that has been the story of Hong Kong's ceaseless quest for building land within frontiers that for half a century were tightly closed. From 1950, when the Communist revolution in mainland China brought the first massive influx of refugees into what was then a British colony (raising its population from 1 million to 2.25 million in a matter of months), until the 1997 handover to the People's Republic of China, the survival of the population of Hong Kong depended on engineering skills stretched to their limit. As a result, from the man-made reservoirs that supply water to its 6.5 million population, to the glistening office towers and sprawling container ports that are the engines of its economy, Hong Kong is the invention of engineering, architecture and design. Even if the force behind its growth wanes, now that the city has become a Special Administrative Region of China

Plan of one of the
principal levels, with
railway station at the
top (below).
Model (right).
View of the new
housing blocks, built
as part of the airport
project (below right).

The terminal's ceiling,
which uses repeating
details over the entire,
vast area (overleaf).

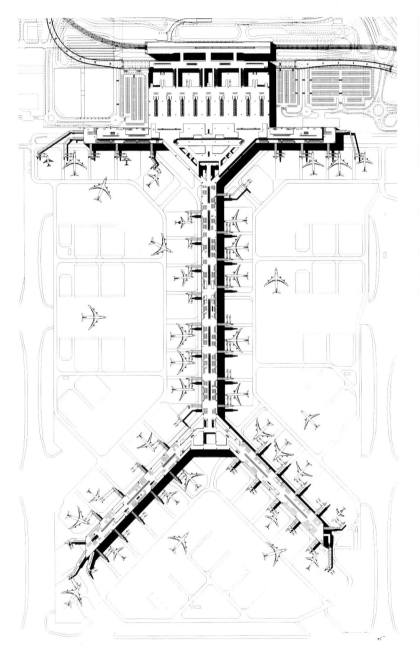

with endless land on its doorstep, for years to come 'slope control' will still be a reminder of Hong Kong's heroic past.

The most recent, and the greatest of Hong Kong's feats of engineering, is the £12 billion airport that has been blasted out of the coastline at Chek Lap Kok, a small island now dissolved into a 21 square-kilometre (8 square-mile) plateau reclaimed from the sea off Lantau Island. Ten years ago this remote outpost, 32 kilometres (20 miles) west of Hong Kong harbour, took two hours to reach by boat. Today, huge slices have been cut out of the topography of the stepping-stone islands of Lantau, Ma Wan

and Tsing Yi to construct a road and rail link that cuts the journey to half an hour. The route is spectacular, incorporating as it does the world's longest double-decker road and rail suspension bridge at Tsing Ma, which carries a six-lane expressway with mass transit railway tracks below it, and enclosed emergency roads on either side for use in typhoons. Together with the mast-stayed Kap Shui Mun bridge that connects Lantau and Ma Wan, as well as associated viaducts and cuttings, these tremendous interventions in the landscape serve as a fitting introduction to the wonders of the airport itself.

The idea of building a new

The repeating curved vaults, which all run in the same direction, and give consistency and a sense of orientation at all points in the building. The roof rises and dips at different places (section, below).

airport for Hong Kong goes back to the 1950s. With the advent of wide-body jets in the 1970s, it was already clear that Kai Tak, Hong Kong's first airport, was approaching the limits of its usefulness. Originally a naval airstrip that was located at the water's edge in Kowloon so as to be under the protection of the coastal defence guns on Hong Kong island, Kai Tak's military role disappeared with the growth in civil air travel after World War Two, when it was repeatedly extended to receive more and larger aircraft. By the mid-1990s, processing nearly 30 million passengers a year, it had become the world's third busiest airport, but its single runway and

death-defying rooftop approach made the title difficult to hold on to. Clearly, any new airport for Hong Kong would have to be considerably larger, with room for two runways, clear approaches and a passenger and cargo capacity three times as great as that of Kai Tak.

### The grand plan

As Hong Kong's economic links with mainland China increased by leaps and bounds after the détente reached by Beijing and the United States, the city became more and more a high-tech service centre for the cross-border industries of Shenzen and the Pearl River Delta. Inevitably Kai Tak became even

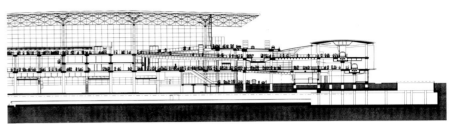

Section through the entrance area (above), showing the connection with the railway station.

more of a bottleneck. The speed and range of jet airliners meant that half the population of the world lived within five hours' flying time of the city. If no action was taken, one or all of the rival Pearl River international airports – Macau, Shenzen and Guangzhou – could steal a march by expanding to absorb the traffic generated by East Asian economic growth as a whole.

As a result of considerations like these, in 1989 the Hong Kong government authorized the construction of a new, twin-runway airport at Chek Lap Kok, coupled with a high-speed link to the city. The executors and supporters of the project – initially not including the

Chinese government – anticipated not only attracting all the pent-up expansion of air traffic in the region, but servicing the needs of commerce and the tourist industry connected with it as well. To this end they planned to mobilize the transport infrastructure of the high-speed link in true Hong Kong fashion. Six new railway stations were planned, each to also act as a platform for retail, residential, office and hotel air-rights developments, which totalled a massive 3.25 million square metres (33 million square feet). To allay the concerns of the Chinese government, it was even envisaged that a vast linear city with a

population of more than 50 million could step off from this link, sweeping north in a great 193-kilometre (120-mile) arc along the rail and auto routes leading to the mainland city of Guangzhou. All the elements of this plan, from the most modest to the most ambitious, depended on the success of the new airport at Chek Lap Kok.

**The passenger terminal**
Although working with only a single runway at the time of its opening on 6 July 1998, the airport that has resulted from this master plan is already the largest and most fully equipped air transport hub in South-East Asia. Key structures

already completed include the widely publicized 1.27-kilometre- (0.78-mile-) long, 550,000-square metre (5,920,145-square foot) main passenger terminal, an associated 55,000-square metre (592,014-square foot) Ground Transportation Centre (the GTC), and a 320,000-square metre (3,444,448-square foot) air cargo complex (called SuperTerminal One), by Norman Foster and structurally engineered by Ove Arup and Partners.

The GTC stands alongside the entrance to the terminal and combines all landside transport systems – car, taxi, bus and rail – under a single unifying gull-wing roof. SuperTerminal One, located

The glass perimeter wall gives a sense of the outside from deep inside the building (left). The rail concourse (right).

south of the passenger terminal, is designed to cope with an annual throughput of 2.6 million tonnes of cargo by means of two automated bulk storage systems and an outrigged automated container storage system that provides nearly 2 kilometres (1.24 miles) of access to the airport apron, the length of airside interface being the principal limitation on speed of cargo handling at many existing airports.

Of these three huge structures, the most prominent by far is the passenger terminal, the largest such building in the world and one of the few terrestrial structures big enough to be visible from outer space. Constructed on eight levels,

only three of which reach out to the full length of the concourse, the terminal obeys the design principle of vertical weight distribution originally applied on a smaller scale at London's Stansted airport (also by Foster and Partners). Accordingly, the heavy rail Automated People Mover (APM), together with all heavy systems and servicing equipment, is confined to the lower level while the three full-length concourse levels are used to separate arrivals and departures. In operational terms, the elongated 'Y' shape of the concourse maximizes the airside perimeter of the terminal so that 38 aircraft boarding gates (a number that will

increase to 48 after the completion of the second leg of the 'Y') can be served in addition to 27 remote aircraft stands.

With all heavy elements confined to the lower levels, and nearly all of its perimeter clad in 21-metre- (68-foot-) high tinted and laminated glass, the most powerful and continuous design element of the passenger terminal is its roof, a remarkable structure that soars over the departures mezzanine and the concourse, its cleanness of line and purity of form unspoiled by intrusive intermediate supporting columns, visually obstructive partition walls or untidy suspended elements. Of deceptively simple

appearance, inside and out, this barrel-vaulted roof effortlessly accommodates changes in height as well as direction as it runs the length of the 1.2-kilometre (0.74-mile) terminal from the cantilevered entrance canopy facing the GTC to the furthest departure gate at the end of the 'Y'. Structurally the roof is assembled from 129 site-welded steel lattice shells, each covering an area of 1,300 square metres (13,999 square feet), its apparent simplicity the outcome of a joint effort on the part of architects and engineers to cut its kit of parts down to the smallest possible number of components, in pursuit of maximum economy and

Underneath the all-encompassing roof, a huge landscape opens up of the airport's multiple activities, including the largest airport shopping centre in the world.

speed. The diagrid structure of the shells themselves is a good example of this, being built up from thousands of identical standard steel beams welded together on site at precise angles on special jigs so as to produce 36 x 36 square-metre (118 x 118 square-foot) assemblies weighing between 43 and 136 tonnes. After construction these huge assemblies were painted *in situ* by mobile spray painting sheds before being lifted by computer-controlled hydraulic transporters and positioned over their massive reinforced-concrete supporting columns. The bolted joints between the shells and the columns were specially designed to absorb large

horizontal and vertical tolerances, so as to accommodate changes of level without needing special parts.

Like the standardization of the lengths of the structural members of the roof, the triangular ceiling panels that conceal the underside of the roof decking also display a rewarding synergy. There are thousands of them, mostly cut to a standard size. They not only fit flush between the welded structural members, but in other locations, close to the rooflights and along the maintenance walkways, they serve as daylight and luminaire reflectors, throwing light back up on to the underside of the roof to give a floating effect.

### Retail is detail

If the palpable size, simplicity and integrity of the interior of the terminal at Chek Lap Kok owes everything to its 36-metre (118-foot) column spacings and the brilliantly designed roof that rests upon them, the exploitation of its tremendous interior volumes derives from the almost open landscape this mode of construction has created. Passengers entering the terminal find the slender post-tensioned bridges across the massive atrium provide an awe-inspiring introduction to the terminal space. Once inside the eight-storey main terminal, which is over 300 metres (984 feet) wide, enormous internal

areas open up. The low-level baggage reclaim hall alone is frequently compared in size with New York's Yankee Stadium, while the concourse-length Automated People Mover tunnel is two storeys deep and as wide as a motorway.

More significant in a different way is the intensive allocation of the retail, food service and hospitality elements at the airport. Close to the entrance, with its 288 check-in desks, is the first concentration of retail outlets. Once beyond this array, departing passengers emerging from passport control on level seven find themselves in the

At the entrance to the airport (below), beneath a portico formed by the projecting vaults, the road connection runs between the terminal and the railway station.

Hong Kong Sky Mart, an even larger retail space that is claimed to be bigger than any other airport shopping centre in the world. This single-level stretch of serviced floor space is landscaped in such a way as to enable it to operate as the equivalent of a town square for the terminal's shifting population. Above level seven on the departures mezzanine are clustered the first- and business-class lounges. These spaces enjoy tremendous outside views and are of an appropriate size for their anticipated population. The Cathay Pacific lounges alone extend to over 4,000 square metres (43,055 square feet) in what their London architect John Pawson describes as 'a building within a building' that is lavishly endowed with restaurants, bars, lounges, spas and reading rooms appointed and furnished with high quality materials including granite, wood, leather and glass (and even a flowing stream) so as to create a luxurious yet also residential atmosphere with private suites equipped with every domestic convenience.

**Reflections**

As the above description suggests, in many ways the planning and function of the passenger terminal at Chek Lap Kok is a microcosm of the pattern of development that is intended to spring up along the Lantau link between the airport and city – and indeed prefigures growth within the city itself by future utilization of the large construction site created by the abandonment of Kai Tak. The issue is not whether this great increase in the upper limit for new serviced floor space will be exploited rapidly or slowly but rather, the certainty that it will be, sooner or later. Change is a constant in the life of Hong Kong, and the speed with which modern times fade into history there is invariably shocking to European eyes. Today, the inlet where the barges that carried the steelwork for Norman Foster's Hongkong and Shanghai Bank were unloaded in the early 1980s no longer exists. Filled in by land reclamation, it is the site of an established small town with its own high-rise apartment towers. No doubt the state of mind bred by 50 years of these metamorphoses goes a long way to explain why the drive for development in East Asia is so strong: stronger by far than the downforce generated by the region's temporary economic woes.

The terminal is to be both a symbol of Yokohama and an extension of its public space, as well as fulfilling its function as a transport building.

# Yokohama International Port Terminal
## Ship of state

Irénée Scalbert

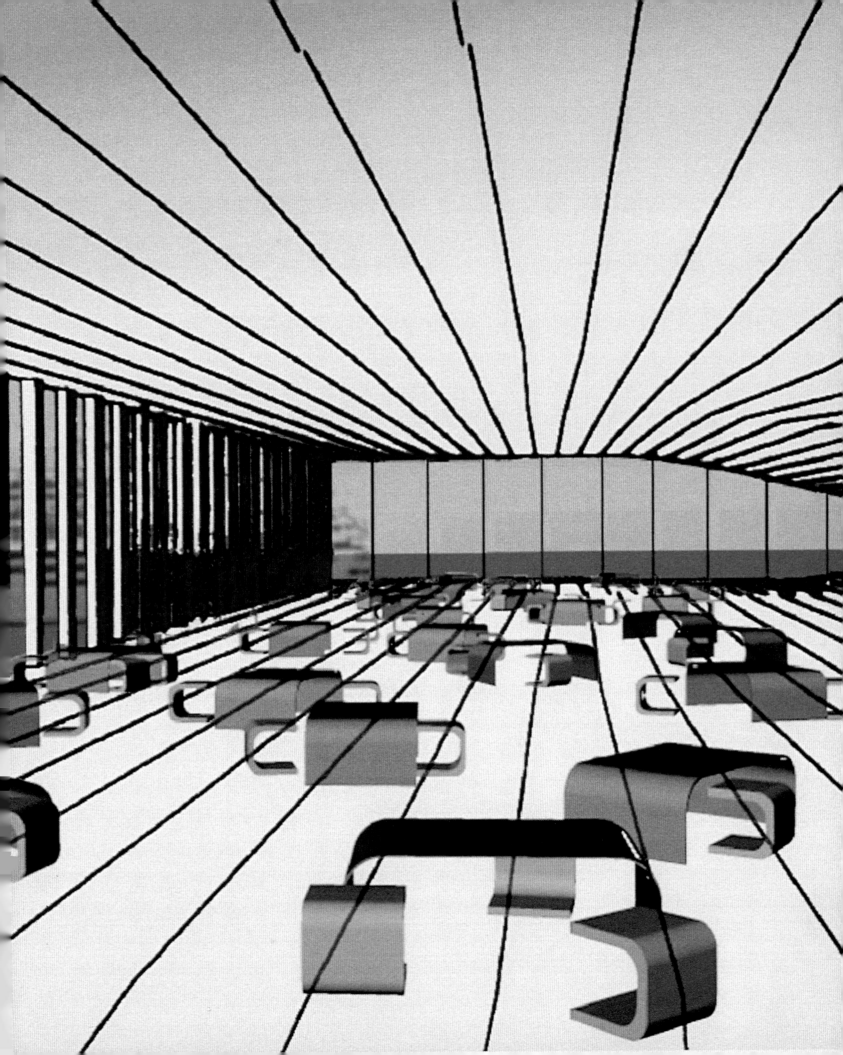

Competitions are not held to promote inconspicuous architecture. The Sydney Opera House, for example, dominates the city skyline with its white, eccentric forms, and the Pompidou Centre rises above the grey fabric of Paris like a giant *tricolore*. These are unforgettable monuments, symbols not merely of their own purpose but of everything that lies within reach of their shadow. New York without the Statue of Liberty, London without Big Ben, Athens without the Parthenon: such prospects are enough to inspire a sense of dread.

When, in 1995, the City of Yokohama organized an international competition for a ferry terminal, what did they get? Selected from more than 700 entries, the winning project by Foreign Office Architects (FOA), appears to contrive a sense of its own absence. At 400 × 70 metres (1,300 × 230 feet), it is large. Yet as described in the architects' perspective drawings, it is low, grey and mostly empty but for a scatter of small unidentified objects, a few people and two or three cars. Next to it, the cruise liner creates by far the greater impression. Were it not for the high vantage point, the oddly warped surface of the roof would itself disappear, leaving nothing to see but a gaping arch lifted from the face of the terminal to produce a smile as enigmatic as that of the Mona Lisa.

The prefecture of Yokohama is the wealthiest in Japan, not least because the greater part of the expanding trade with China passes through the city's port. The site for the new terminal, on a pier, is adjacent to the city centre, which commands the highest land values in the country. Reaching far into the water, it is set within the southern fringe of the harbour bay, between Yamashita Park to the east and Red Brick Park to the west, where old warehouses are being renovated. It lies on an axis with a large baseball arena to the south. Physically prominent, the pier is also significant for its history. It was here, in the nineteenth century, that Western seamen were first allowed to land in Japan. The notoriety of the site will be further enhanced when cruise liners, such as the *Queen Elizabeth II* and the *Crystal Harmony*, dock along its sides.

The design is likened by its architects to a *millefeuille*, but it compares more accurately with a stack of fried poppadoms. The upper leaf is at once traffic interchange, access court and public promenade. This plaza,

108

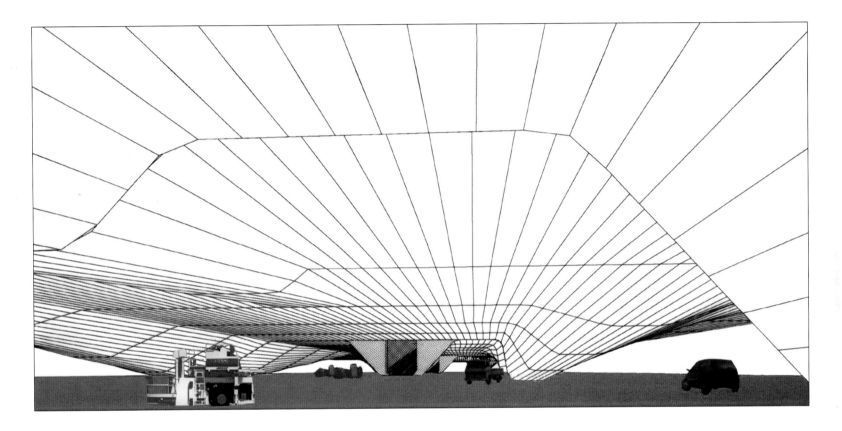

which starts at the level of the existing pier, gradually swells upwards to a modish peak of 15 metres (49 feet), thus limiting the impact of the building within the landscape of the bay. To avoid introducing columns in the interior and to preserve the continuity of the structure, a series of pleats were formed in its surface to provide support, create spatial differentiation and accommodate ramps and travellators to serve all floors of the stair-free building.

The level of the boarding fingers (the footbridges spanning between ships and terminal) – fixed in the competition brief to 5 metres (16 feet) above the apron of the pier – determined the level of the main floor. A ramped, scallop-shaped forecourt links the south end of the pier to the main entrance. The terminal zone extends some 200 metres (656 feet) behind it, across the full width of the site. It divides into two halls, the first for domestic cruises, the second, beyond passport control, for international travel. Each is slightly domed and is flanked by ramps leading to entrances on the roof plaza. Travel facilities – luggage retrieval, check-in, information desks, and so on – are aligned along the sides, and ancillary spaces, ranging from restaurants to administration rooms, provide the necessary occlusion between public halls and the boarding decks, which are thinly stretched along almost the whole length of the building.

Departing from the brief, the architects placed the facilities destined for local use at the far end of the pier, which invites visitors to walk across the roof plaza, as well as makes the best of harbour views. Few surfaces in this part of the building are horizontal or even symmetrical, and all are cut by ramps at close intervals. At the level of the terminal, restaurants have been designed to take advantage of the views, while a shopping centre is buried inside the plan. The topmost facility is the emphatically named 'Salon of Civic Exchange' which – so the adjoining exhibition hall leads one to assume – will perform well as a commercial convention centre. This last section is accessible by foot via four cuts in the roof plaza, or by bus from a drop-off point at the apron's far end.

At first, a single-storey basement car park was proposed, encased in concrete. It was later raised to the apron level, which saved on digging and waterproofing, and brought it

**Entry to the cruise terminal from the traffic plaza (below). The building's section is constantly changing, with surfaces that are floors in one place becoming ceilings in another (facing page).**

nearer to the terminal. As a result, visitors will afford an uninterrupted view of the building's underside, between the colossal pleats camped on the flat surface of the pier. Beyond the security screens enclosing the car park, they will get glimpses of the service yards and ships beyond, rather like parking in an airport next to the runway. The rows of parking spaces are slightly inflected to accommodate the base of the pleats and, in the central area, to make room for enclosures, where dogs will bark away the boredom of quarantine.

Each space has, in accordance with its purpose, a specific size and form, which are progressively altered to link with the size and form suited to the adjoining spaces. A surface that is a floor in one space sometimes becomes a ceiling in another. Spaces that are high enough to allow for standing in one place taper out into nothing in another, provoking interesting discussions between client and architects concerning the definition of usable space. For example, within which budget should one include the many areas with a height lower than the commercial datum of 1.2 metres (4 feet)? These last were classified as structure expenditure, necessary to the stability of the building,

their cost being partly offset by savings resulting from the absence of columns. The architects at first envisaged a structure made of corrugated steel, which mimicked the spatial idea of the building. The engineers employed by the City of Yokohama have most recently proposed a dull grid of steel beams of varying depth to match changes in form. Hopefully a bright idea will be found – one that is at once imaginative and efficient.

Taking its place among the large structures of the harbour, the building should be as tough and functional as a ship or a warehouse. From the start, the

architects intended that all surfaces, inside and outside, be clad in 'raw', unpainted steel, the roof plaza being coated with rubber as is common practice on the floors of oil rigs. The client favours timber decking which, ironically, the architects at first ruled out for fear that it would be too costly. In turn, the additional expense enabled FOA to argue – against the wishes of the client – that all internal surfaces should be left unplastered, which would leave the steel exposed.

The competition brief requested two or three sunken gardens within the building. FOA offered instead the whole roof as a

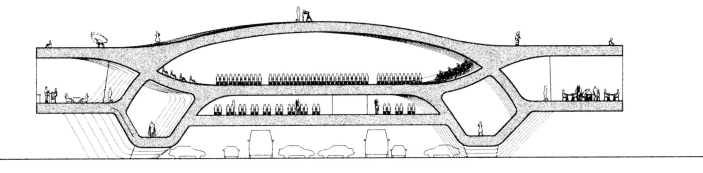

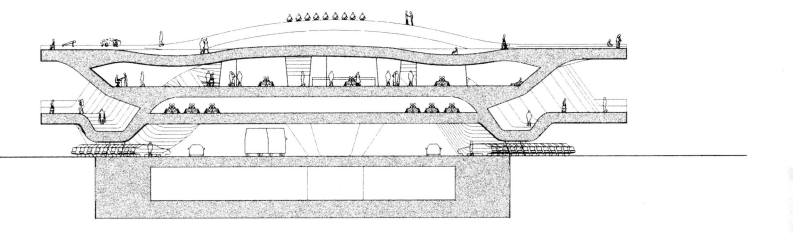

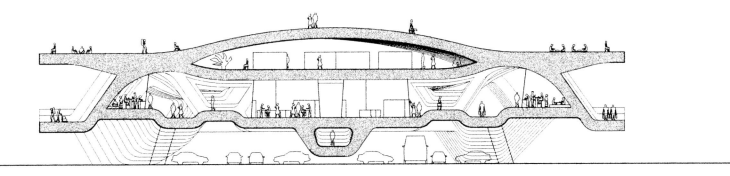

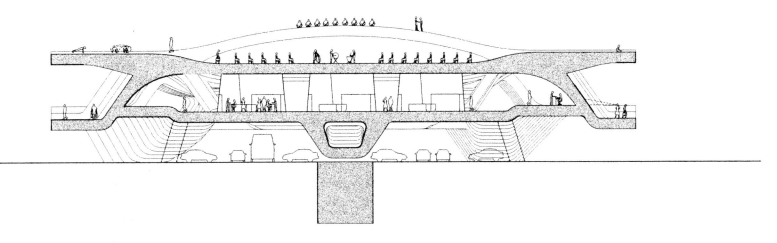

111

The brief requested
sunken gardens,
but Foreign Office
Architects proposed
that the entire roof
be used as a plaza or
garden (previous
page).

park or a plaza. Though clad in timber throughout, its texture varies. It is made rough in places by using a smaller width of plank and by inserting non-slip metal stops and by laying boards in alternate directions. Studs of the kind currently used in Japan for the guidance of the blind delineate paths of a maximum gradient of 12 per cent. Furniture is sparse: included are benches, tilting lamp-posts stood perpendicular to the shifting roof plane, raked auditorium seats, bus stop shelters in the forecourt and allowances for as yet unknown future uses (called 'traces of events'), such as fenced areas for

basketball training.

Like the pioneers of functionalism in the 1920s, but now assisted by computers that bring a higher definition and speed to the design process, FOA seek a perfect match between programme, space and structure. The use of computers, the architects claim, has made the traditional 'parti' – the early commitment to an idea that governs every subsequent decision – irrelevant. In the age of computerized information, the insertion of new data and parameters automatically brings about a new configuration of the whole. This they refer to as an

'add-in' process, in which information is integral to the 'diagram', or basic form of a project, unlike the old 'add-on' process which simply verifies the initial idea.

What seems right in theory is often complex in practice. At first, the architects used a geometry consisting of 'spline' curves, in which the displacement of a particular point affects the position of every other point along their length. This, it would appear, describes an 'add-in' process by which an infinite number of curves is generated. At competition stage, an already impressive 25 sections across the

building had been produced, each one different from the next, and some 100 had been included in the feasibility study. Each time the client required an element to be moved, such as a ramp, four or five sections had to be redrawn in both directions. Simplification became urgent, and as a result the architects were forced to work not with spline curves but with 'complex' ones, which can be split into discreet segments, each with its own radius. As a result, it became possible to limit the number of curves to seven, and to modify parts of a section without substantially affecting the whole, describing an 'add-on' process. It

Facilities for the use of Yokohama's residents, such as the 'Salon of Civic Exchange' (below), are placed at the far end of the terminal, encouraging people to make full use of the structure.

Geometrical analysis of the terminal (overleaf).

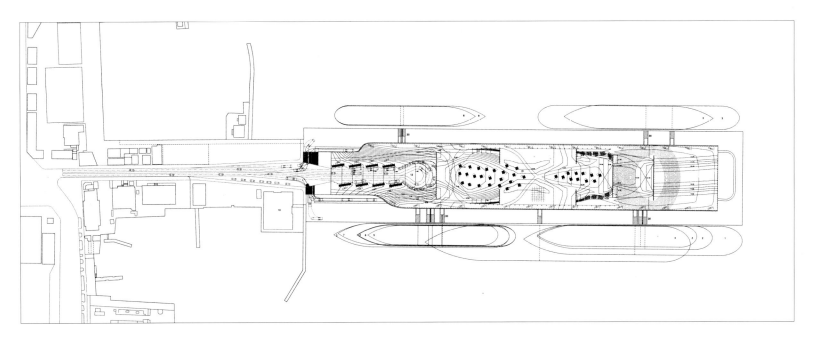

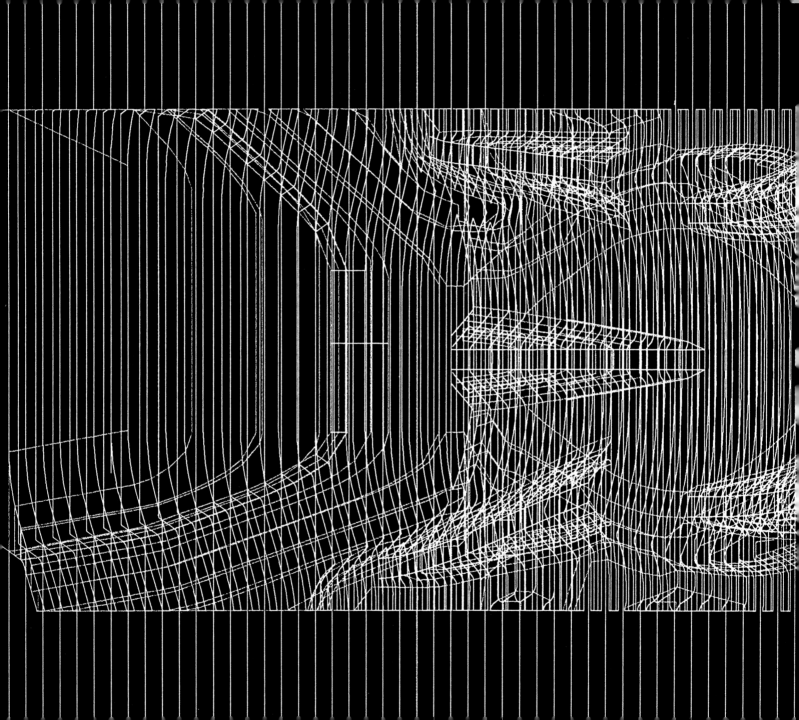

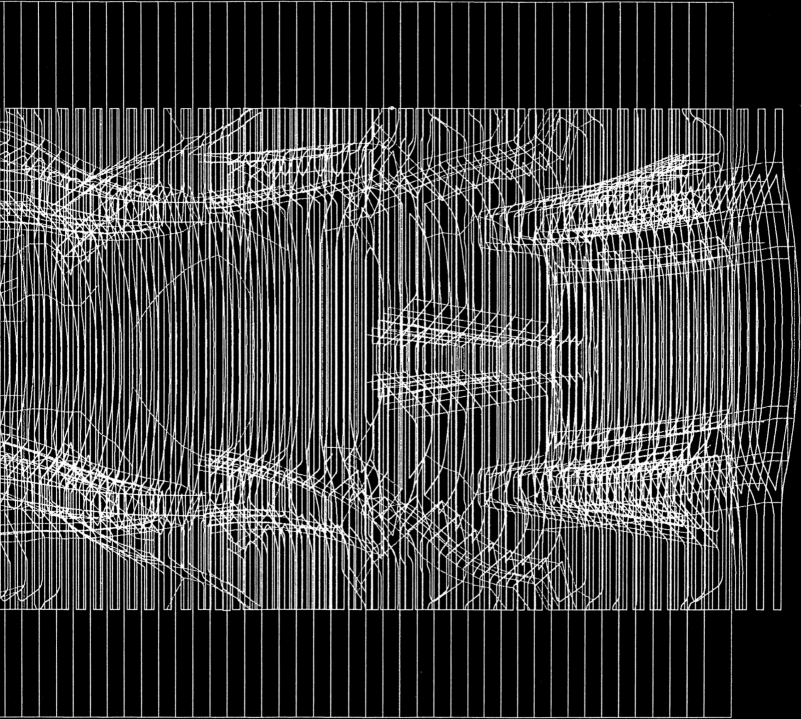

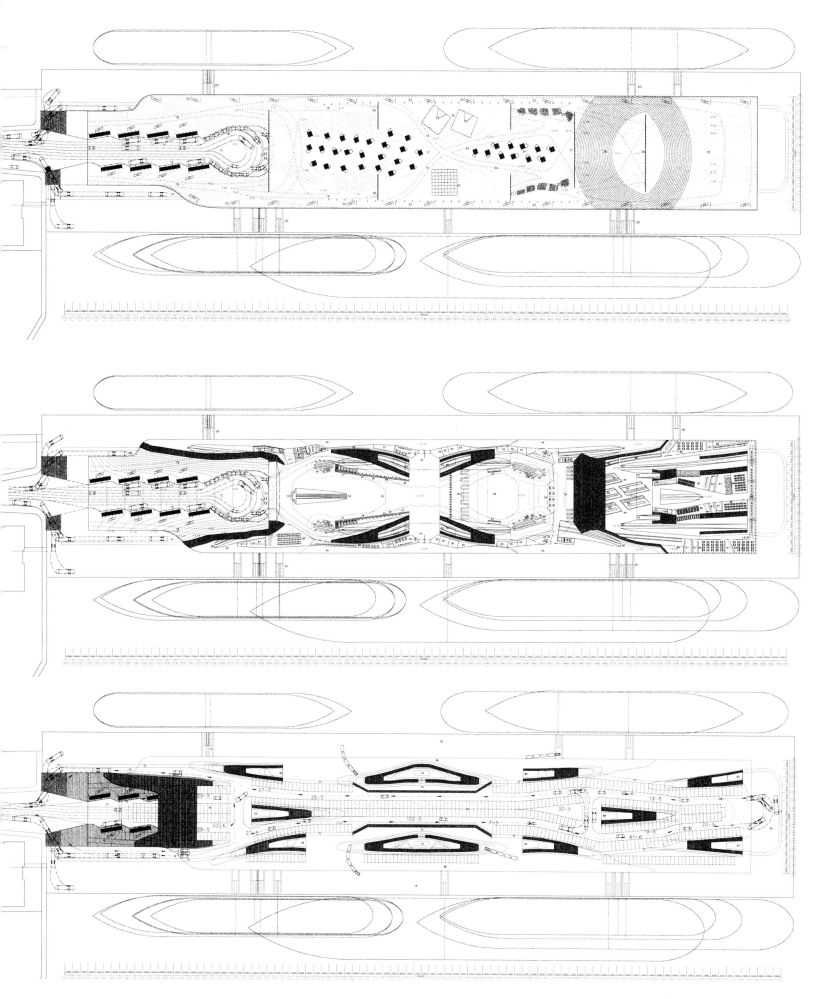

The terminal repeatedly bifurcates in plan and section, offering different ways of circulating round the building (below).

Plans (opposite, from top to bottom): the roof plaza, terminal (restaurant level), and apron level.

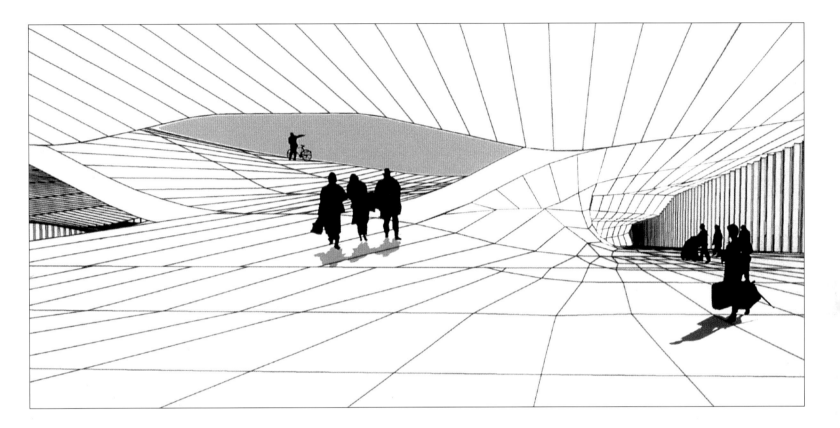

seems, therefore, that the more information is added in, the greater the pressure to adopt add-on methods. Since 1995, the project has wriggled like a fish on the apron of the pier and, say the architects, 'we do not know when it will stop moving'.

The brief is no more set at the time of writing although the architects have recently confirmed that it will go ahead, and FOA will need much flexibility. In 1995, the cruise industry was growing and a ferry terminal seemed a natural choice for Yokohama. Studies later revealed that Japan, due to its harsher climate and high cost of living, was a less desirable

destination than the Caribbean. The recent loss of value of the yen, however, has made Japan competitive with many European cities, and it has brought about fresh interest in the cruise industry.

The city, however, needs neither the commercial returns nor the enhancement in passenger capacity that such a building might bring. The project represents for the City of Yokohama far more than a ferry terminal. It is hoped that the building will direct international attention toward Yokohama, thus adding to its importance nationwide and beyond. The real

value of the terminal resides in its design. The Landmark Tower, built by Mitsubishi across the harbour, may be very high, but it is conventional in design terms. The ferry terminal, on the other hand, is a far more potent sign by virtue of its strangeness. It has become a monument in waiting, as memorable and symbolic and pointless as the giraffe that, won by Napoleon during the campaign of Egypt, made a triumphant journey to Paris.

The authorities of Yokohama appear to want FOA's sensational architectural effect regardless of purpose. The architects, for whom the design is anything but a

monument, at one stage studied the option of breaking its structural surface into facets. But the client insisted that it should remain the smooth object that won them the competition. If the project is in its conception about disappearance within the flows that bring life to the city, the client values its very opposite: its far-reaching architectural presence and its monumental fame. It is hard not to side with them when the ultimate prize could be a place of compelling beauty, comparable in scale to the Tuileries Gardens in Paris, bound along its sides not by the frontage of the rue de Rivoli, but by some of the greatest ships in the world.

# Private housing

**The creation of a lake in the Nevada desert enabled the creation of lush golf courses.**

# Lake Las Vegas Resort
## Just add water

Paul Davies

A promotional brochure shows the good life to be had at Lake Las Vegas Resort (left). Housebuyers have the option of choosing standard plans, decorated with their own selection of additional features (below).

Peering across the desert on a scorching afternoon in the autumn of 1832, you might just have spotted a thin haze of dust on the horizon, a pack train of Spanish and Mexican traders hurrying toward Las Vegas Springs, man and beast craving water and the shade of undisturbed meadows.

It would take another 40 years before a tiny ranch was established in this land of nomadic Paiute Indians, and 20 more years before you might view a tiny transient settlement of prospectors, rounders, garrotters and thieves mixing inconspicuously with teamsters, swampers, saloonmen and railway construction workers creating a town called Las Vegas.

Forever transient, whether trading post, gambling town or the world's greatest holiday resort, from campsite to a city of 100,000 hotel rooms, it has proved hard to imagine people actually living in Las Vegas, making homes there.

But today, it is not the hollow ring of picks on rock that resounds

through the hills outside Las Vegas, but the satisfying clunk of 'Big Bertha' titanium drivers against two-piece compression-moulded G-Force golf balls. Civilization has arrived, and it is not the grimace of hard labour that furrows the brow, but a missed putt on the 13th green.

Lake Las Vegas Resort is more than a residential community. It is a 'living master plan' with its centrepiece a 130-hectare (320-acre) man-made lake, built from scratch in the desert a half-hour's drive from the Las Vegas Strip. The pioneers staking their claims on the initial phase of 360 custom and estate homesites set around its southern shores will enjoy exclusive use of Nevada's first Jack Nicklaus-designed signature championship golf course at the foot of their gardens. They will be paying up to $2 million for their 0.2 hectare (half-acre) desert plot, or 'homesite', and more than $2 million for a custom home. Lake Las Vegas Resort is the latest incarnation in a tradition of gated

communities where golf is integral to the concept of living, where the ranch is the golf course, by now the dominant model for new homes in the far west. In particular the famous Spanish Trail community in western Las Vegas, home of the Las Vegas leg of the PGA golf tour, established this model in Nevada. But Lake Las Vegas Resort is altogether a more extravagant, mesmeric moment in our consideration of the desert, and its transformation to dreamland.

Into the millennium, Lake Las Vegas Resort – for which the lead architects are Nichols, Brosch and Sandoval Architecture – will grow to include a little piece of Italy called The Village of Monte Lago, offering a luxury hotel designed as a facsimile of the Florentine Ponte Vecchio; office space; a 9,000-square-metre (100,000-square-foot) retail plaza; and a European-style casino. A Hyatt Regency Resort will transport guests to a 500-room sultan's palace, surrounded by a Nicklaus-designed resort golf

course. Lining the 16 kilometres (10 miles) of exclusive shoreline will be an additional world-class golf course, Mediterranean-style residences, where rocky outcrops are substituted for verandahs, pantiles and terracotta plant pots and the desert floor populated with gleaming Lexus saloons and 4 × 4s, laid with acres of imported turf, beds of violets and golf tees.

'Fabulous' Las Vegas's latest addition starts, predictably, with what many would regard an inconceivable proposition; that there should be a lake in the desert. For Las Vegans, the converse is true. In a typical rush of boundless enthusiasm, Lake Las Vegas Resort is marketed as 'two billion years in the making'. The desert was once, after all, ocean bed, so how reasonable to create once more a lake! With the notorious absence of clocks, Las Vegans paradoxically exhibit a heightened sense of time, their average length of residency in the city being less than the maturity of a bottle of blended

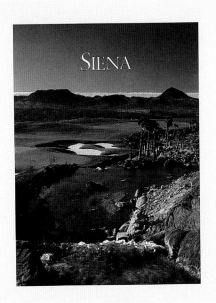

SIENA

The resort's Mediterranean theme extends to the names given to its different districts, such as Siena and Marseilles. The development is planned around Jack Nicklaus-designed golf courses.

Scotch. As Las Vegas exploits our little weaknesses, and exhaustively rebuilds itself to satisfy them, Lake Las Vegas Resort represents a miraculous compensation, exhaling bright lights for calm waters, the inhospitable desert for the glories of nature, Sodom and Gomorrah for the Garden of Eden.

Work created the west, but leisure now sustains it. You no longer have to herd cattle to be a cowboy. Just along the highway from Lake Las Vegas Resort, between 1929 and 1935, up to 5,000 men toiled long and hard, deep in Black Canyon excavating 9 million tonnes of rock and replacing it with 7 million tonnes of honeycomb-framed concrete to create the Hoover Dam, a monument to our will to tame nature, and to sweat. Resulting from the will to produce industry and agriculture, this epic monument to the industrial age provided recreational pleasures as boats took to the resultant Lake Mead, and electricity was made available to Las Vegas Strip, to burn

bright neon and drive the air-conditioning units.

By contrast, Lake Las Vegas Resort, 3.2 kilometres (2 miles) from Lake Mead, does not appear to be the consequence of physical labour, and has no visible infrastructural support, save for ranks of water sprinklers. Lake Las Vegas's engineering and ecological marvel manifests itself miraculously, mysteriously, overnight! Its marvellously produced brochure for

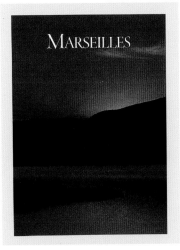

MARSEILLES

Lake Las Vegas Resort includes images of mountain streams, of fishermen in boats, of birdwatchers, of skiers, hikers and golfers, and not a single picture of a house.

As late as 1997, there stood little more than a small visitor's centre in rustic style, decked out inside with promotional models, architects' impressions of this new 'Florence', videos promoting lifestyle and a little picturesque verandah out back where you could stroll to survey the surrounding scene. On the southern shores the first golf course was already open, with its clubhouse in Mediterranean, but also vaguely Frank Lloyd Wright, style. There was little else but bare rock, a large expanse of water, and a sense that something sublime was going to happen there very soon.

Any nostalgia for the homestead, for the shack in the desert, for towns with desperately optimistic names like Hope, Arizona, is inappropriate for Lake Las Vegas, where the individually parcelled communities have

European, metropolitan names like Barcelona, Marseilles, Monaco and Siena. The promise is Venice without fog, Florence without rain.

Arriving via McCarron, America's fastest-growing airport, Lake Las Vegas Resort is a cruise south down Highway 95 to the soft rumble of rubber on concrete, out over Paradise Valley with its distant mountains gazing at the monstrously lush billboards, poised way up on huge grey steel skeletons, which advertise Lake Las Vegas Resort as 'The Wonder of Nature, The Imagination of Man', to tunes on the radio – no longer those of a lonesome Willie Nelson, but of a vivacious Vivaldi.

The route marked by these great totems, towards Henderson and the Hoover Dam, runs past Henderson's monumental magnesium plant (supplier of the incendiary cores to American bombs in World War Two); past its tidy centre (a field of slowly taken traffic intersections); and up into the foothills towards a sudden flash of nature perfected.

When complete, the civic centre will reflect the Mediterranean theme with its references to Italian architecture (below).

A left turn on to the perfectly manicured boarders of Lake Las Vegas Parkway, where lush turf, flowers and shrubs trail off into the desert highland, past a fieldstone marker with polished gold lettering, assures that you have finally arrived.

Secure in Lake Las Vegas Resort, you have found your destiny, geographically, physiologically and economically. The inhabitants will be the maturest of baby boomers, those who have enjoyed the fruits of the west's flourishing post-war economy (but have tired of Los Angeles), or younger brasher CEOs from industries relocated to Las Vegas seeking a quality of life to match their aspirations and achievements, and some tax breaks.

At one time, the prospect of gold in the hills – or on the baize-covered tables – brought with it a physical relation to tools, the immediacy of the cowboy with his pack. Contrary to sweat, striking rich in these rocky outcrops now corresponds to canny manipulation of the global stock market. This effort, it seems, demands, paradoxically, more space for recovery.

Comfortable settlements in the desert have traditionally appealed to the retired. The early days of this phenomenon were marked in 1960 with the establishment of Sun City, the first exclusive gated community established for retired people outside Phoenix, Arizona. Families, it seemed, no longer fragmented as the youngsters left home, but when the mature elders decided to cash their chips and move on to a better life. Las Vegas has made this migration especially attractive, with a financial climate that contains no state, corporate, or personal income taxes, and no state inheritance tax.

Lake Las Vegas Resort broadens the appeal of the desert settlement as retirement home by appealing to those with still-bulging appointment books and global schedules, whose idea of the global village translates neatly into a timeshare golf villa. Meanwhile, a

characteristic of today's mature and successful is to feel permanently invigorated and youthful, so images in the promotional brochures show predominately middle-aged and younger inhabitants. Besides Las Vegas being well practised in the fulfilment of dreams, it has a keen eye on the older generation: with them come grandchildren to visit, while mum and dad enjoy their adult pleasures and spending power on Las Vegas Boulevard.

The developers for Lake Las Vegas are the appropriately named Transcontinental Corporation, under the leadership of Ronald F. Boedekker, joined by the interests of Sid and Lee Bass, and famous for similar developments in Scotsdale, Santa Fe and Hawaii. Henry Gluck is co-chairman of Transcontinental Properties, ex-chairman and CEO of Caesars World, and is personally credited as the architect of the recent expansion of the casino monoculture into a hinterland of retail experiences, as well as the transformation of gaudy Las Vegas

Strip into smart Las Vegas Boulevard. At Caesars World, he created Forum Shopping, one of the most successful shopping malls in the world, in the belief that once his customers had done enough gambling in the casino, shopping was as natural a way to relax as taking in a Las Vegas show, and considerably more profitable. Lake Las Vegas Resort is a natural extension of this principle, and a significant moment in the transformation of a monoculture of casinos into a balance of provision, capitalizing on a range of desires, from the thrill of the next card to the peace of the perfect dream house; a totalizing, seamless, corporate synergy.

The project is managed via a chain of development teams. Individual owners create custom homes with teams of selected architects and designers, within guidelines set for the Lake Las Vegas communities. Protection against over-development is guaranteed by the unique status of this piece of

**When complete, the resort's retail, hotel and casino complex will reflect the Mediterranean theme. The hotel will span the water, housed an a version of the Ponte Vecchio in Florence.**

desert as development land. The surrounding publicly owned lands are untouchable. Isolation increases the sense of repose.

The architecture of the custom home, notwithstanding the exuberance of the Ponte Vecchio in The Village of Monte Lago, is a distinctly American combination of taste and style. Within certain guidelines, established by Lake Las Vegas Resort developers, plot owners interview and assemble their development-team of architect, landscape and interior designer, and home builder. 'Character' and 'warmth' within the desert setting and Mediterranean styling (almost ubiquitous across the West Coast) are highly valued. However, a custom home, the peculiarities of which are mediated by taste, is not like a custom car, whose individualities are moderated by opportunity. In Lake Las Vegas Resort, conformity is the rule; while each client, for the professionals involved, is unique,

their custom home responds to individual lifestyle choices. The result is a sublime combination of evenness and 'individuality' that characterizes the sophistication of this American culture.

The dawn sky once boomed with the retort of military aircraft, and even nuclear explosions: now both have been silenced. The interiors of the city of casinos would resound to the incessant high-pitched chime of slot machines and the low mumble of the craps pit boss, punters were 'hopped up' for four nights and crazy with it. If anybody lived here at all, they were castaways, degenerates of every persuasion, or vampires of the night. Now, in Lake Las Vegas Resort, under starlit nights normal folks sleep soundly, embracing security, favourable tax conditions, and relief from the Los Angeles traffic.

Serenity, the fullness of time, the abundance of time, and the opportunities to fill it, makes Lake

Las Vegas Resort a very special addition to the fastest-growing middle-size city in America. Las Vegas never stands still, it flickers and adjusts like the electronic fuel injection of a very, very thirsty engine. In a wonderful (and equally synthetic) compensatory device, Lake Las Vegas Resort now contemplates eternity. And for that eternity, what was once considered barren desert becomes the Garden of Eden, a place of innocence. Beyond the responsibilities of business, life is expected to re-establish our childlike state of perpetual wide-eyed innocence in the face of nature. Viewing the scene from the mountain trails cut into the landscape around the lake, barren rocks transform into a 'natural wonderland' with opportunities to spot and photograph exotic birds, previously witnessed 'only in natural history magazines'. Within the lake, a 'paradise' of fishing awaits, with stocks of

rainbow trout and large-mouthed bass.

Stranded in the Mojave Desert without water, your life expectancy would be three days. Now, in Lake Las Vegas, water is abundant. It is not a question of hope, as it was for the settlers in Hope, Arizona, but one of quiet satisfaction. On your arrival at your 'homesite', you will have swapped the rumble of concrete under your tyres for the smoothest, freshest, black tarmac, swept past entrance gates and warning signs, through security, past the manicured, landscaped borders, past the rows of sprinkler devices, caught a glimpse of Nevada's biggest man-made lake, and gazed over the rocks and appreciated the beauty of their 'muted palette of warm reds, deep browns, rich crèmes and subtle tans'. Standing on the raft foundation of your dream house, consuming these signs floating in the massive space of the desert, crack a soda; you have arrived.

# Public housing

**Kazuyo Sejima's slender housing blocks achieve a high degree of lightness and transparency.**

# Gifu housing, Japan Reversed planning through gender

Akira Suzuki

132

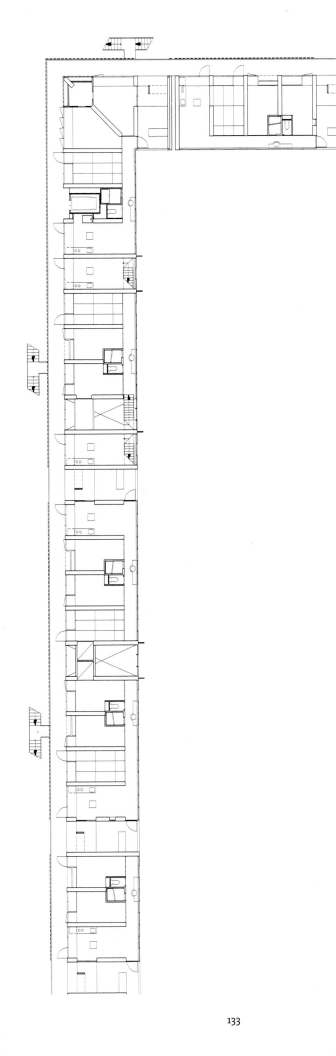

**The washbasin occupies an unusually prominent position within the typical apartment (following pages).**

The most startling aspects of Kazuyo Sejima's architecture are to be found in her residential projects. Those who have visited Sejima's housing, either as a professional or an amateur, are astonished to find such minimum style: using man-made materials such as polycarbonate panels destroys the expectation of cosiness and intimacy found in the usual home environment. The question is whether these high-tech materials can successfully function in a domestic context. Professionals have criticized the durability and high maintenance of these materials, as well as their ability to protect against the elements.

The translucency, lightness and neutral atmosphere inherent in many synthetic materials – unburdened by the associations embodied in traditional Japanese substances like wood or paper – creates a feeling of accessibility. Despite the presence of these visual qualities in most contemporary Japanese architecture, Sejima's works have been much acclaimed and have attracted a great response from the young generation via the media and magazines. This following is based on the individuality of her housing, which in turn stems from her unique treatment of the plan. These housing schemes do not adhere to a rationale established by other contemporary architects, though visually her buildings share common aspects with them.

Gifu High Town Kitagata is sited in the suburbs of Gifu city, in between Nagoya and Kyoto: a typical Japanese scene of supermarkets, small houses and rice fields. The housing project was organized by the Gifu Prefecture and coordinated by Arata Isozaki in 1994. Isozaki commissioned four women architects – Christine Hawley, Elizabeth Diller, Akiko Takahashi and Kazujo Sejima – to each design one block. His master plan is intriguing both for its confrontation of practical issues and its application of the gender theme to public housing.

Let's have a look at Sejima's plan for her block of flats in this public housing development. On the opposite side of the south opening, depending on the size of the flats, either two or three bedrooms are set next to each other. Adjacent is the living room, which includes an open-plan kitchen and dining area providing access to the flat's main entrance. The open terrace runs from north to south and is located on the opposite side of the wall to the living room. All the rooms are arranged next to one another, divided by the same uniformly arranged structural spanning walls. These structural walls run parallel to each other through the flat in a north–south direction. The rigidity of construction methods and materials has produced a puzzle-like, random elevation. In the eyes of critics, the grid pattern recalls a prison façade.

The view from the public corridor to the north side of the flats is of doors. The number of doors you see depends upon the number of bedrooms in each flat. Screens and staircases are made in zinc-plated expanded metals. These inorganic materials, together with Gifu's austere design, do not evoke a sense of kindness, friendliness or even pleasure in the dwelling. (The materials chosen for this project are not the result of cost limitations, although Gifu is a low-income

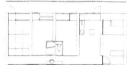

public housing scheme.)

Christine Hawley's block, in a maisonette style, has entrance halls for each of her flats comprising a large void. At the block designed by Elizabeth Diller, a movable screen has been incorporated, so that space can be altered to suit the tenants' various and changing requirements. The idea for the estate to consist of ten-storey-high buildings was a requirement of Isozaki's master plan. This maintains a protected courtyard in the middle of the housing, surrounded by buildings that have the maximum possible internal space. A parking space has been given for each flat – a rare arrangement in Japan. It would have been possible to build these blocks to half their height: clearly, the costs for these estates are higher than that of the average housing block elsewhere.

## The bedroom with no daylight and the washbasin in the sun

The intention behind the design of the bedrooms, constructed from equally lined spans, becomes clear once you enter the flat. The plywood flush doors, which separate the bedrooms from the rest of the flat, look like doors to storage spaces. The bedroom has been designed so that it receives little direct sunlight once the door is closed. The usual design of family housing, comprising individual, intimate bedrooms, has not been used here.

Sejima's placement of the washbasin within the flat defines her approach to the scheme. It is installed at the south side of the flat, facing a large front window. You wash your face, apply your make-up and dress while facing this large opening. It is possible to think that such activities should be done in the privacy of the bedroom or the en-suite bathroom, as accommodated within the plan of

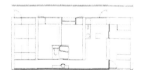
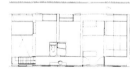

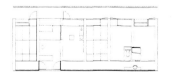

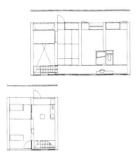

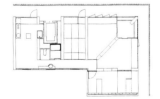

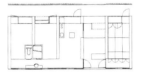

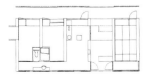

traditional Japanese housing. In contrast to Sejima, Christine Hawley has planned her flats in a manner where the basin is concealed from view. In so doing, the washbasin area has become a very restricted space. In Hawley's flats, a small basin and bathroom have been placed, with the bedrooms, on the upper level. The lavatory is on the lower level, next to the living room. Hawley's maisonette-like plan is seen to be the more relaxed – and conventional, from a Western perspective – of the two.

**The family as a unit**

Catering for the needs of the nuclear family has been the main concern of public housing throughout the twentieth century, despite its shifting agendas. Influential examples of this concern can be found in the Siedlung Georgsgarten by Ernst May, the Unité d'Habitation by Le Corbusier and social housing estates in Britain such as that at Roehampton. The comfortable standard of living to which social housing aspires has encouraged low-income citizens and their families to stay within the city, which in turn maintains the city's flow. Social housing exists for this purpose, among others. Contrastingly, social housing in Communist Russia was designed to aid the efficiency of its workers, resulting in the prioritization of the individual, as opposed to the family unit. Individuals were encouraged to live off their social support, regardless of their family.

In recent years, Japanese architects such as Toyo Ito, Riken Yamamoto and architects of the younger generation, including Sejima, have been continuously studying social housing for single-person occupancy (Yamamoto's houses, for example, usually consist

of separated individual spaces, rather than rooms connected beneath a roof). The outcome of their research suggests plans where the individual room is connected directly with the outside, rather than layouts that focus on the internal life of the family.

In Japan, the demand for 'one-room mansions' – concrete boxes containing studios with a kitchen and a bathroom – has exceeded the demand for traditional, small wooden houses. These 'one-room mansions', together with *Konbini* (convenience stores), evolved to make living in the city easier for the single person.[1] One argument says that the demands of the modern city constructed these environments before architects suggested the styles of living.

However, Sejima's housing in Gifu is not targeted at this lifestyle. According to the Public Housing law, the purpose of social housing is for low-income residents who live together as a family and who have problems obtaining accommodation of their own.[2] Sejima does not ignore these conditions, or try to force a family to live with a plan intended for single-person accommodation. Rather, it caters for family members' freedom of movement: the doors to each room open on to a corridor with direct public access, so that there is no need for individuals to pass the living room on their way out.

**The reversed family: housing plan by gender**

The washbasin in the sun is stunning. Standing in front of it feels like you are standing in front of the whole world. In reality, there is another block opposite, which means the user is, in effect, facing society. Washing your face used to be done behind closed doors. This activity is now in full view and brought to public attention.[3] Thus lies the importance of Sejima's strategy: the housing block has been designed around the activities of the 'daughter', who is treated, through the plan, as the principal person in the family.

The middle-aged male, the father who used to be the master of the house, may use the washbasin twice a day, as would his wife. But the family member who always keeps their best face to show in public is the 'daughter'. All the toiletries are hidden behind the basin in the centre of the flat, and there is nothing to hide from the outside world. The intention behind this planning becomes clear: the activities that are traditionally done behind doors – washing the face or doing the laundry – are now openly presented to the public, and are placed in a position of prominence at the front of the living space.

Let's have a look at the plan again. Although the washbasin is in the sunny south-facing section of the flat, the space is directly linked to the living room, where the kitchen and the main entrance to the flat are placed. The terrace, which is the most open part of the plan, includes a laundry space that leads through from the living room. The links between inside and outside are opposite to the traditional conception of the plan, like the inside out of a jumper you have thrown to the floor. Maintaining her face (physically and metaphorically) is a very important activity for the daughter of the house.[4] The daughter's face is projected on to the centre of society. It makes sense to have this space in the centre of the flat, in full view of the public's attention, where it can be easily accessed when returning from outside. In Japanese contemporary society, more high-school students

('daughters') use mobile phones than any other section of society. Talking about private matters on mobile phones in public places demonstrates the way that the boundaries between public and private space are becoming closer.

There may be a chance for the middle-aged man to become the main user of the flat if he removes his suit and tie (symbols of a social and domestic status almost without meaning in contemporary society). However, Sejima's revolutionary plan does not try to rule or force its residents to change their lifestyle. The issue that Sejima is aiming to prove is that a nuclear family does not necessarily have to stay as a nuclear family, or even produce another one.

Isozaki, as master planner for the housing project in Gifu, decided to select women architects with the aim of reorganizing the plan of the flats, rather than the family unit itself. Sejima found a creative answer to solve Isozaki's gender theme. The key was the generation of the plan through the daughter as the focus of the family unit. A daughter who is not, in our present society, guaranteed to produce another family herself. She may be a part of the family for now but may not be in, say, ten years' time. The question is: should such an unstable, fragile part of the family become a key part of the planning process? More traditional householders may say 'no'. That's fine! But I would like to ask one more question: how many years of your life do you think that your experience of your family will last? I hope that your answer is longer than 40 years, which is the maximum durability of a standard Japanese building.

*Translated from the Japanese by Yuri Nakamura*

**Notes**
1. *City Life from a Four and a Half Mat Perspective, 4+1/2: The Internal Landscapes of Tokyo*, A. Suzuki, Harbour Front Centre, Toronto, 1995.
2. The Public Housing law was established in 1951 when the region's Public Organization built 'lease' houses. Currently, this form of housing exists all over Japan (in about 3 million cases) and comprises 13 per cent of all rented homes.
3. Sejima placed a washbasin in the sun at Saishunkan women's dormitory, completed in 1991. An iconic example is Corbusier's washbasin in the entrance hall at the Villa Savoye (1929–31), which stands as a symbol of cleanliness and health, at the same time signifying modern life.
4. In 'Untitled Film Still #2', Cindy Sherman captures the private moments of a young girl in front of a washbasin. See also N. Lahiji and D. S. Friedman, *Plumbing: Sounding Modern Architecture*, Princeton Architectural Press, 1997.

The Shanghai World Financial Center, due to be the tallest building in the world, will crown the forest of towers in the new district of Lujiazui.

# Shanghai World Financial Center
## Love and rockets in the spree economy

Aaron Tan
Louise Low

To visitors, the winding avenues of neon en route to Shanghai from the bustling Hongchiao airport may advertise the distinctly commercial sensibility of this mega-city of 14 million inhabitants, but nothing can prepare them for the visual centrepiece at the waterfront, a concrete, glass and steel 'big bang'. Shanghai is in the middle of a huge make-over, and as the biggest and most cosmopolitan city in China, it has propelled itself into the front ranks of the country's long march into the neon-capitalist age. With a nod from Deng Xiaoping, since 1990, the capitalist floodgates have been flung open and money has poured in with a momentum that is as unstoppable as the water surging through the Yangtze gorges toward the sea.

Shanghainese officials boasted not too long ago that one fifth of the world's cranes were employed in this city, which has seen, between 1992 to 1996, growth rates surpassing 13 per cent each year. Within seven years in the newly developed Pudong (West Pu), across from the legendary Bund (the man-made embankment), over 150

skyscrapers will sprout out of gray fields and smog-choked factories. Between 1994 and 2000 Shanghai will have built 7 million square metres (75 million square feet) of office space, equal to today's entire stock in Hong Kong, according to some conservative estimates. However, like all best-laid plans, there is always a monkeywrench waiting to be thrown into the works: in the rest of Asia, the second half of 1997 saw the burst of one economic bubble after another, many of them swollen like an emphysema on the hot air of real estate boom. Will Shanghai be next?

In comparison with much of the rest of Asia under the current economic malaise, Shanghai looks positively robust. Round-the-clock construction continues on skyscrapers throughout the city and nowhere is the pounding of piles more palpably felt than at Lujiazui, Pudong's designated finance and trade zone.

### Architectural pyrotechnics versus cinderblocks

In 1992, an international consultation on Lujiazui Central

The great circular opening at the top of the World Financial Center (left) was to have contained a Ferris wheel. Now it will have an observation deck. Lujiazui, with the Eastern Pearl Television Tower on the left, and the Jin Mao Tower in the centre (far left).

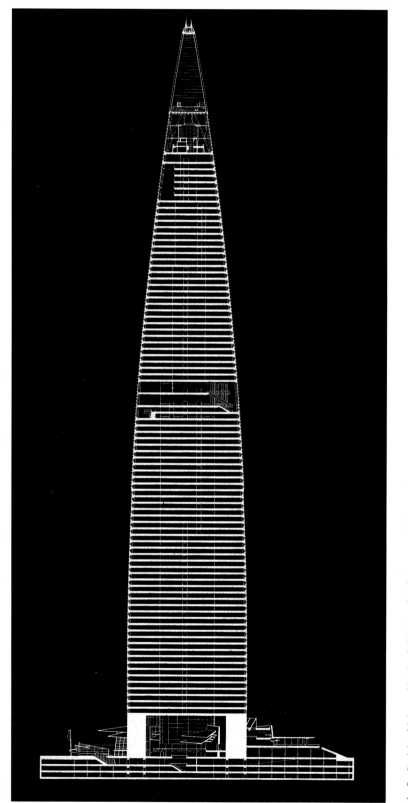

Area planning and urban design was held, jointly sponsored by the Shanghai municipal government and the French Ministry of Public Engineering. Five consultants, Rogers from Britain, Perrault from France, Fuksas from Italy, Ito from Japan and the Shanghai joint team presented projects. While the Shanghai municipal government insisted that the final master plan be an amalgamation of the unique and outstanding attributes of all five schemes, it is clear from the contrast between the foreigners' idea of Shanghai and the Shanghaineses' own that they were at cross purposes. Ironically, what stands out most is that which is missing in most of the other foreign teams' schemes: an echo of the Bund across from Pudong and a Manhattanesque skyline of ornate vertical edifices.

The Shanghainese worship their Bund. Each day, they arrive in large numbers for their morning and evening routine, be it for contemplative t'ai chi, raucous ballroom dancing or a romantic stroll. In more discreet corners huddle the mendicant, the starving scholar, the laid-off state workers and the shabby sojourners from the countryside, looking for work and bearing placards narrating their all-too-familiar life stories. Unfailingly, all of them will, at some point, pause and take in the sight at the waterfront, famed in the 1920s and 1930s for its towering skyline, the most spectacular in Asia.

Some of the consultants' proposals centred monotonous blocks of humbler stature around a large open public space resembling a piazza. They offered an urban equivalent of the Grand Canyon when the Shanghainese were looking for a Mount Rushmore. Toyo Ito's proposal for a luminous and transparent flux at ground level topped by monolithic square blocks arranged in neat rows is more in step with the grandiloquent Shanghainese sensibility. Ultimately, the Shanghainese opted for a plan that arranges a radial three-dimensional conurbation of skyscrapers, each with its own unique pompadour, in such a way that the view of the Bund across from the city is maximized for each tower. Those closer to the waterfront are obliged to build lower and more horizontally, or to tilt at an angle. This Chinese logic of urban negotiation also extends to generous gestures to developers for their sacrifices: those who have been bound by height restrictions are 'compensated' with a small adjacent patch of public green.

Even as urban plans undergo careful deliberation, developers are given carte blanche to pursue their florid metropolitan dreams. Lujiazui's architectural flamboyance defies categorization with its phantasmagoria of shapes, colours, height and metaphors, clustered over a relatively compact site. This is set amidst a complex of state-of-the-art infrastructure – tensile steel bridges, elevated highways and invisible underground rails – and punctuated by the huge Eastern Pearl Television Tower. A rocket-like structure skewering several silvery balls straight out of a 1950s sci-fi B-movie, the tower's mind-boggling design makes postmodern sense since, television – bless its iridescent cathode-ray heart – is, above all, an escapist construct.

In the July 1998 issue of *Wired* magazine, Bruce Sterling marvelled

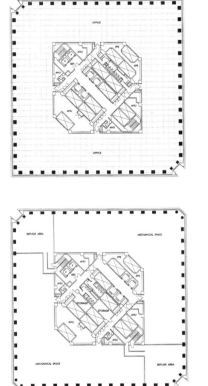

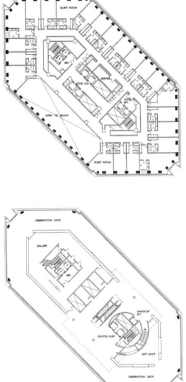

that: 'The Shanghainese have skyscrapers with saucers, geodomes, cupolas, balconies and big weird wings. There are buildings crowned with monster Statue of Liberty hats and with *Flash Gordon* ray-gun emplacements. Shanghai's new art museum is built like a giant bronze pot, including the handles. The new stadium has a U-shaped roof – an upright U, that is. You gasp in awe, and then you giggle.'[1]

Sophistication with a touch of vulgarity is, of course, very much the Shanghai way. Add to this panorama of incandescent exposure a blizzard of outsized neon icons of Asian consumerism – Coca-Cola, Kodak, Sony, Nissin Cup-a-Noodle – atop giddy buildings with names like 'Sun Come Building', and the spectacle of this dream city of unbridled capitalism is complete.

Lording over the architectural cacophony is the kingpin-to-be of all skyscrapers: the Shanghai World Financial Center, at a majestic, 460 metres (1,509 feet) and sweeping 94 storeys. Commissioned by the Japanese giant developer, Mori Building, and designed by the US corporate architecture heavyweight, Kohn Pedersen Fox Associates PC, the building has moved on to the second stage of its construction, after engineers pummelled about 2,000 steel piles into the earth bank, some as deep as 80 metres (262 feet), according to Kiyoshi Yoshikawa, Mori's overseas publicity counsellor.

Expressing a buoyant optimism in the face of the relentless tsunami of bad economic tidings (seas of debt in Asia, plunging stock indices, downward-spiralling currencies, massive capital flight) Yoshikawa is

confident that 'good buildings in Shanghai are competitive, in short supply and will enjoy high occupancy.' With pundits predicting that the current 50 per cent vacancy rate will rise to 60 per cent by the end of 1998, Yoshikawa sees his company's investments bucking the trend:

'Ours are Grade A buildings and even in these difficult times, many Grade A buildings in Shanghai have an occupancy of 80 per cent. The government has been moving much of its operations from Puxi, which has its own limitations, to Pudong. The Shanghai Security Exchange Building is in fact almost fully occupied. Shanghai will continue to witness an influx from other commercial organizations, Chinese or overseas, looking to establish their regional headquarters here.

'The Shanghai World Financial Center will be a multi-use, state-of-the art building with diverse facilities for offices, a hotel, shops, banks, observatories and a museum. It is an "intelligent" building and will function like a vertical city. We foresee a huge potential in attracting overseas investors who are looking for offices in Shanghai, including those from the G7 nations.'

In 1996, the monthly rent of some buildings was US$8 per square foot: in 1998 it has dropped to US$2 per square foot, and is still not attracting tenants. What fans the unwavering faith and stoicism to see the construction of the world's tallest building through, early in the next millennium?

Shanghai isn't just any ordinary Chinese city, insists Yoshikawa, and China, with the enormous size and heterogeneity of its population, culture and resources, isn't any

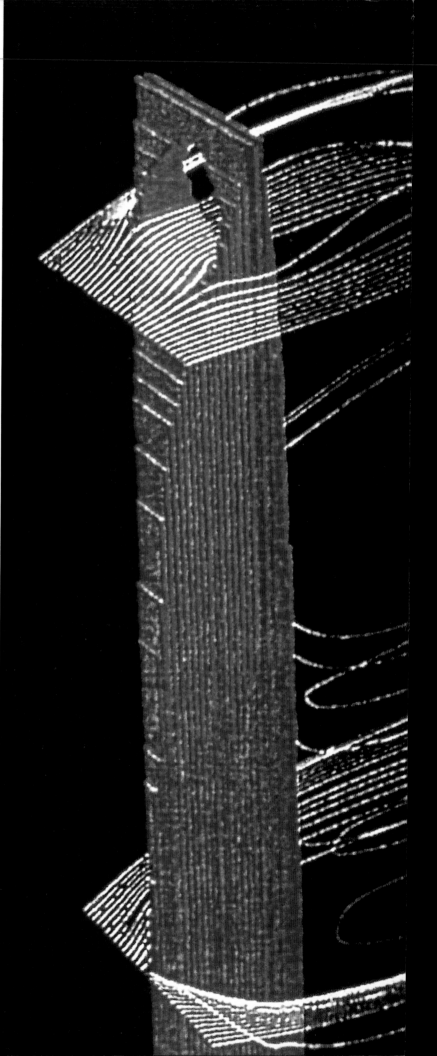

KPF, the architects of
the World Financial
Center, treated its
exterior as a
sculptural excercise,
experimenting with
models to find the
preferred shape
(previous page).

ordinary nation:
'Shanghainese are typical of very aggressive Chinese in the pursuit of knowledge and learning experience. They have a positive attitude towards technology. In addition, they have a history of sophistication in international dealings and particularly good business sense and human resources.'

Shanghai's strategic location with the enormous Yangtze hinterland of over 400 million inhabitants is one more oft-quoted reason for this optimism, and the staunch political support of Shanghai's own prodigies, the current two most powerful politicians in China, is another. Nonetheless, brave new investors who are no pikers when it comes to Shanghai's future, find themselves inevitably gravitating to Shanghai's own myth of a past.

**Paris of the East; whore of Asia**
By Chinese standards, Shanghai is a young city, having come of age in the twentieth century. After losing the ignominious Opium Wars at the end of the nineteenth century, a humiliated China ceded Shanghai to various foreign concessionaires – the Americans, English, French, Germans and Japanese – who promptly got down to the business of making money. Shanghai's population swelled from 50,000 in the mid-1850s to 3 million by the 1920s, in an outrageously accelerated boom that would make today's Lujiazui look like a laggard. The simultaneous demographic crossing and economic expansion have produced radical modifications and social consequences. From the start, Shanghai's vocation was moneymaking; its idol was Mammon and its heart lay wholly in the market place. A journalist noted in an old issue of *Fortune* magazine that 'if, at any time during the Coolidge prosperity, you had taken your money out of American stocks and transferred it to Shanghai in the form of real-estate investments, you would have trebled it in seven years.'

If half the stories about pre-World War Two Shanghai were true, this sink of iniquity would have long since lapsed into the South China Sea from the sheer weight wrought by the collective indulgences of the millions of degenerates reported to have lived here, drowning enough libertines and criminals to make a pontoon bridge of bodies all the way to Hong Kong. The eastern ridge of this ancient Mandarin country would simply not support the plummet of prostitutes, gangsters, bankers, merchants, opium-addicts, pimps, politicians, artists, intellectuals, fugitives, vagrants, thieves, lunatics, sadists, tourists and human chancres of every description.

An early, albeit less highbrow progeny of the current vogue in architectural programmatic indeterminacy may be found in some of Shanghai's more notorious high-rises, the tallest buildings in the world outside of Manhattan at that time. Hollywood film producer Josef von Sternberg visited Shanghai in the 1930s and wrote about the infamous Great World Amusement Center in his book *Fun in a Chinese Laundry* thus:
'The establishment had six floors to provide distraction for the milling crowd, six floors that seethed with life and all the commotion and noise that goes with it, studded with every variety of entertainment Chinese ingenuity has contrived:

The World Financial
Center's shape is in
part generated by the
need to reduce wind
resistance, modelled
on computers.

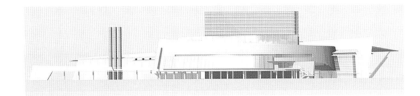

The World Financial Center's deconstructivist base contains a shopping area, a lift lobby and parking.

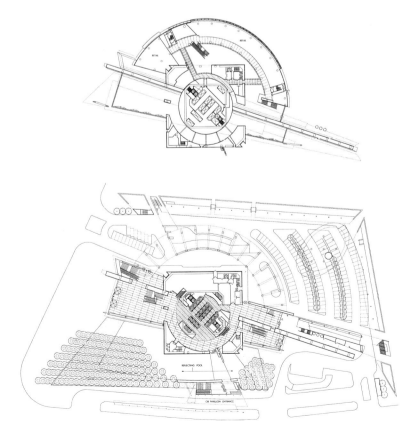

'On the first floor were gambling tables, singsong girls, magicians, pickpockets, slot machines, fireworks, birdcages, fans, stick incense, acrobats and ginger. One flight up were the restaurants, a dozen different groups of actors, crickets in cages, pimps, midwives, barbers and earwax extractors.

'The third floor has jugglers, herb machines, ice-cream parlors, photographers, a new bevy of girls – their collared gowns slit to reveal their hips, in case one had passed up on the more modest ones below who merely flashed their thighs – and under the heading of novelty, several rows of exposed toilets.

'The fourth floor was crowded with shooting galleries, fan-tan tables, roulette wheels, massage benches, acupuncture and moxibustion cabinets. The fifth floor featured girls whose dresses are slit to the armpits, a stuffed whale, a storyteller, peep-shows, balloons, masks, a mirror maze, two love-letter booths with scribes who guaranteed results, "rubber goods" and a temple filled with gods and joss sticks.

'On the top floor and roof of that house of multiple joys, a jumble of tight-rope walkers slithered back and forth, and there were seesaws, lottery tickets and marriage brokers. And as I tried to find my way down again, an open space was pointed out to me where hundreds of Chinese, so I was told, after spending their last coppers, had speeded the return to the street below by jumping from the roof.'[2]

Paris of the East, whore of Asia, queen of the Orient, pearl in the East, this place was a myth-maker's paradise, so vast, so varied and heavy with thronging humanity that the imagination is tempted to run wild at the sight of it. This instinct to anarchy is inevitable. It's the only possible reconciliation between humanity's best instincts and worst realities. By the end of the 1970s, half a century of invasions, civil wars, great leaps forward, revolutions and other social convulsions had drained Shanghai's spirit, and the city lay sore and afflicted in a state of nightmarish reverie.

In the post-Deng 1990s, Shanghai appears to be swinging again, its denizens discarding their Mao suits and transforming themselves from revolutionaries to card-carrying members of the international consumer mainstream. Today, there are 22,000 foreigners in Shanghai, compared with 100,000 in the 1930s, but they keep streaming in. The city's notorious appetite for carousing has again been rekindled, from expensive restaurants and cabarets to cheap discos and karaoke bars that are often thinly disguised brothels, with names that hedge heavily on the city's past: the Cotton Club, Shanghai Sally's, Blues and Jazz. Nothing is more Shanghainese than an excessive open-handedness (*kuo sho*), ostentation and a tendency to often vulgarized showiness and swagger. For the newly arrived yuppie, lifestyle, entertainment, recreation and shopping are all wrapped up in a single debit solution against a shiny new Visa card. Shanghai is in a rush to claim its rightful place next to Paris, Tokyo, New York and London – or will it be Kuala Lumpur? It either is, or isn't, the wave of the future.

**The millennium scourge – the metaphor of technology as fetish**
The twilight of the twentieth

century is witnessing the dawn of technomania, courtesy of the typical breathless hyperbole rhapsodized by Toffler quoting opportunists, bottled and sold to self-styled 'visionaries' from Al Gore to Mahathir. When the millennium comes a-bugging, it is suddenly not enough for cities or societies to be of the moment or 'in' it. The AT&T promise 'YOU WILL' delivers us into this mythical future. The future is already a cliché.

The search for the urban equivalent of the 'killer app' precipitated such titanic adventures as Malaysia's futuristic Putrajaya, a digital wonderland programmed to tap into the lucrative tech/biz/ culture global venture capital vortex. With hyped-up project names like 'Multimedia Super Corridor', these are new cities dreamt up for the sole purpose of attracting the digital vanguard, in the hope that a handful may turn out to be future Bill Gateses.

Likewise, the high-tech ambitions of Lujiazui send architects scrambling to find futuristic metaphors of unbridled optimism for their high-heeled office blocks. While the architecture appears to be steel-and-concrete flights of fancy, there is in fact an underpinning technological reality. Shanghai is home to more than its fair share of rocket scientists. Here, at a shed-like factory in the Minhang District, Long March rockets are designed and manufactured in increasing quantity and precision alongside a popular brand of refrigerators. The Shanghai Aerospace and Refrigerator Factory is considered one of the finest in China, with a success rate that had US Pentagon officials squirming in their seats.

However, instead of seeing the kind of pork traditionally forked out by governments, the factory supports its space-age products with the manufacture and sale of its refrigerators. Perhaps one day a Chinese expedition to Mars will be made possible by the wholesaling of advanced washing machines and dryers that do not swallow socks.

Every ready-made city ever built, from Brasilia to Putrajaya, has suffered from artificial showcase architecture at the expense of pragmatism and function. Many failed to meet their society's expectations – the promised economic miracle never materialized, the powerful futuristic myths they were designed to project having turned to kitsch. The feeling of living in a bureaucrat's imagination and the utter meaninglessness of its hype is precisely what these new metropoles are all about: completely of-the-moment, all mood and no meaning.

Has good old Chinese sense and rationalism, which has served the country for over two decades, been overridden by the folly of the parvenu, whose self-portrait will be immortalized in asphalt, concrete and diamond-cut glass? Will the critical mass of 14 million forward-thinking Shanghainese be enough to attain the escape velocity needed to transcend the fate of other 'instant' cities? Beyond the privileged discourse of 'experts', perhaps no one (neither journalists nor governments) but the Shanghainese themselves know how they will appropriate the city, harness the technology and in the process, learn how to interface with the future and change the boundaries of the possible. As they once did.

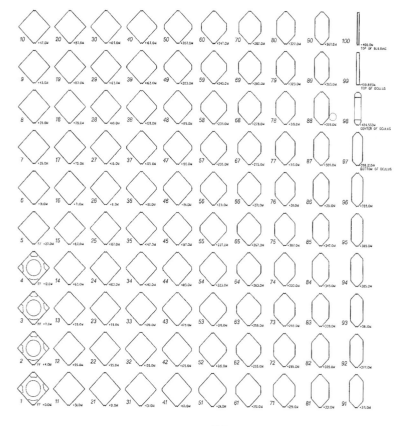

**Notes**
1. Bruce Sterling, 'The Spirit of Mega', *Wired*, July 1998, p. 162.
2. Quoted in T. Johnston and D. Erh, *Western Architecture in Old Shanghai*, Old China Hand Press, 1993.

# Spectacle

# The Millennium Experience, London
## A dome – yet different

Deyan Sudjic

Throughout its history, the British state has, unconsciously more often than consciously, attempted to represent itself through its buildings, its insignia, and its artefacts. Indeed, the very concept of Britain – now under question with a sharpness that it hasn't had to face for more than 300 years – is a construct designed to provide an accommodation for the Scots, the Welsh and at least some of the Irish with the English, offering a single supranational definition of national identity. This is an identity that is clearly a fabricated artefact, in which architecture has an important role to play. Specific buildings become the symbolic landmarks which define that identity and the architectural language of these landmarks becomes the medium by which this identity is propagated.

The process of the creation of such identities has become increasingly methodical and deliberate since the beginning of the nineteenth century. The rebuilding of the Houses of

Parliament after 1834 was perhaps the most obvious example of the British state representing itself through architecture with the knowledge that it actually had a conscious stylistic choice to make. The decision to build the Millennium Dome is nothing less than a deliberate attempt to create an equally powerful and equally charged symbolic landmark. But such clear-cut decisions are rare in Britain. Other European states have been less reticent about addressing such questions. François Mitterrand, throughout the 1980s, deliberately set out to make Paris the dominant metropolis of a unified Europe through a building campaign that consciously echoed Haussmann and Napoleon III. It was a campaign that adopted an architecture of simplified geometric forms and the aggressive use of steel and glass to symbolize a certain view of France.

Until the late 1990s this approach has not, by and large, been one that has found much sympathy with the British political

elite. During World War Two, there was a parliamentary debate after the destruction of the House of Commons' debating chamber about the most appropriate means of its reconstruction. Members argued in favour of a modern chamber as an assertion of a dynamic and vigorous Britain emerging confidently from the trial of war. But the eventual decision, supported by Winston Churchill no less, was to invite Sir Giles Gilbert Scott to reconstruct the chamber in the manner of Pugin and Barry. It was hardly a surprise.

Contrastingly, the assumption of power by the Blair government has seen an unparalleled degree of political interest in the imagery of architecture and design, calculated to show the British state in terms of its modernity. This presents an apparent rupture with the unstated assumption that it is the duty of British governments to present a façade of continuity. There is in this rupture a clear echo of the self-conscious youthfulness of the no longer derided 1964 Wilson

administration with its embrace of technology and popular culture. Tony Blair, after all, wasn't the first prime minister to bask in the reflected glory of rock stars.

But the bruising impact of events such as the collapse of the Lloyd's insurance market and the Barings Bank debacle are also significant. These are events that show British traditions in their worst light, and may in retrospect have represented nothing less than a paradigm shift in notions of the essence of the British identity. Lloyd's was the essence of British enterprise, before it bankrupted its small shareholders, marrying coffee-house traditions with high-tech architecture. After its crash, Lloyd's seemed to demonstrate that an outward adherence to traditional values represented only sclerotic stagnation.

The new political class in Britain has certainly learned the lessons of François Mitterrand's *grand projets*. Immediately on assuming office in May 1997, the Labour Party

**The Millennium Dome is, like the Houses of Parliament, an attempt to use architecture to represent the British state.**

embarked on a well-prepared campaign to represent Britain as a dynamic and youthful commodity. It was a campaign that was both about symbolism and, in theory at least, substance. The representation of the state was an issue, but so was the perceived economic impact of promoting design and architecture.

No single building has embodied this preoccupation as clearly as the plans to commemorate the millennium with a massive structure on the Greenwich peninsula. Formerly 120 hectares (300 acres) of toxic Victorian dereliction, the site is now occupied by the most highly charged piece of political architecture in England.

Curiously, despite the current identity of the Dome as the very embodiment of New Labour, this was a project that was set in train by the then Conservative Prime Minister, John Major. It was the Conservatives who initiated the Lottery, which is paying for it, and it was the Conservatives who had the

idea of celebrating the millennium by allotting one fifth of the public yield from the Lottery to the Millennium Commission. It was the Conservative deputy Prime Minister Michael Heseltine, who, more than anybody, pushed for the idea of a rerun of the Great Exhibition of 1851 and the Festival of Britain of 1951 to celebrate the year 2000.

And yet this astonishing enterprise has, with remarkable speed, become irrevocably identified as the centrepiece of the New Labour project. Such inter-party promiscuity is new for Britain. The Festival of Britain was instigated by an old Labour government, and opened begrudgingly by a Conservative one that went on to tear down all its physical legacies, save for the Royal Festival Hall, as soon as it decently could. The adoption of the Dome as a New Labour project is all the more surprising since it was a scheme that could have been cancelled without the slightest political risk. Blair chose to embrace it, against

the firm opposition of the Chancellor of the Exchequer, Gordon Brown. Indeed, it might have been precisely because his great party rival was against the scheme that Blair backed it.

The germ of the idea that eventually led to the Dome had its genesis in a series of conversations among the Millennium Commissioners as they toured the country in 1994, dispensing largesse to such unlikely projects as a scheme to garnish Portsmouth harbour with a giant water feature, while refusing to fund Zaha Hadid's design for an opera house in Cardiff. Two Commissioners in particular, Michael Heseltine and Simon Jenkins, believed it was essential to create a single national focus for the millennium. Where and what this might be remained open questions. These informal conversations had to run the gauntlet of the tortuous methods of public procurement. In spring 1995, two separate but interrelated tendering exercises were conducted, one to select a site

for the festival, and the second to select an operator for the project, under the delusion that a private-sector organization would be prepared to take the risk of mounting such an operation. By the end of 1995 the role of operator had boiled down to Imagination – the remarkably successful company established by Gary Withers, specializing in laser and dry-ice launches for new Ford cars – and either Greenwich or Birmingham as the site.

But Withers never had any intention of taking on the financial risk of becoming the operator himself. And British Gas and English Partnerships, the successive owners of the Greenwich peninsula, between them ensured that Birmingham's bid to stage the celebration in a revamped National Exhibition Centre came to nothing. Greenwich could claim to be close to, if not actually on, the meridian line – a feature allegedly of some significance in celebrating the millennium – even if the

international date line might have a more obvious claim. Above all, it had a vast amount of land that needed to be rescued from dereliction. British Gas, which then owned the land, and English Partnerships, the quango charged with brown-field regeneration, asked Richard Rogers to prepare a master plan for the site, and to coordinate a millennium exhibition with Withers. It was a project that clearly could only be delivered by a public-sector body. But the pursuit of the private-sector mirage went as far as the Millennium Commission begging British Airways to take on the running of the project. Withers's original idea had ingeniously sidestepped the content issue by suggesting that it would be up to the people of Britain to decide on it. The exhibition would be the result of shipping the raw material around the country for two years in order to involve the whole of the UK in shaping the final show.

The Rogers proposal, accepted by Jenkins and Heseltine in May 1996,

was to put all this stuff (the shape it was actually going to take could safely be left until later) under the all-embracing shelter of the Dome. That way at least the show could open in December 1999. Worked up into a planning application in October 1996, permission was duly granted for the scheme three months later. As a result, English Partnerships bought the site in February 1997 for £20 million, finally committing tax payer's money to the project.

Then of course came the election. Even before May 1997, Michael Heseltine had been making representations to Tony Blair about a future Labour administration adopting the Dome. A host of soon-to-be obscure Labour politicians weighed in against the extravagance of the project. Even Peter Mandelson says he almost killed it off because 'he was concerned at the rudimentary state of content development'. Gary Withers bowed out, picking up £6 million in fees. But the project never

really wobbled. It was the most obvious means of celebrating the achievements of a modernizing new government, and this was a new government that was determined to celebrate its achievements. Construction started in July 1997 and the first mast went up in the following October.

The official budget for the project stands at an expenditure of £758 million (£466 million is allocated to building costs; the remainder to operational, marketing and contingency costs), financed by a forecast of £150 million in sponsorship, £209 million from commercial revenue and disposals, and £449 million in cash from the Millennium Commission. Of this commercial revenue, £50 million will be paid back to the Commission. This sum does not however include the cost of site acquisition, or decontamination. When this is counted in, the cost of the project amounts to over £905 million.

No British government has been

more conscious of the imagery of power than New Labour, nor more keenly aware of the impact on the electorate of its symbolism. Thus it can only be because New Labour sees enormous potential political advantage from a successful Dome that they have chosen to invest so much party and personal political capital in it. Yet it is inconceivable that they could have realized just how obsessive has been the press's interest in the project, and how vitriolic has been the reaction to the gradually evolving spectacle of the Dome, its management, and most of all, its content.

The Dome has gone through a rollercoaster of different and often conflicting objectives and goals. It began as an attempt to harness the market at the tail-end of Thatcherism, and turned into an almost entirely publicly funded key symbol of the first Blair term. It was conceived of as an attempt to provide a vision of the future, and yet, according to the Dome's one-time creative director, Stephen

**From autumn 1997 to the summer of 1998, the Dome's structure was erected with remarkable speed (see pages following).**

Bayley, even before he quit, the Dome was a fundamentally 'quaint' idea of an expo in the nineteenth-century tradition of the Great Exhibition.

The Dome was intended to be a privately run project that would cost the public sector nothing. Indeed, the prime minister has actually claimed that it was 'not costing any tax payer's money'. He must have forgotten the £147.5 million from the public purse that English Partnerships has poured into site clearance. The House of Commons Arts, Media and Sport committee chaired by Gerald Kaufman was told that expenditure of this level would 'not represent value for money judged purely against the agency's usual regeneration criteria'.

Equally, Blair is glossing over the fact that the Millennium Commission stands behind the Millennium Experience Company with unlimited liability for its losses. If visitor numbers are significantly below the 12 million

predicted, this will leave a substantial revenue hole that will have to be covered by the Lottery. As critics inevitably point out, EuroDisney attracts 10 million visitors a year. The sponsorship target of £150 million is enormously ambitious, though if it is achieved it will earn the millionaire sports agent Mark McCormack a handsome £9 million.

Tony Blair's government has had the longest political honeymoon of British politics, in large part thanks to its deft understanding of the resonance of symbolism at every level, from the death of the Princess of Wales onward. Hence the careful selection of the Royal Festival Hall to celebrate his stunning victory on 1 May 1997, with D: Ream blasting out over the loudspeakers as dawn rose over the Thames, together with the clutch of millionaires showing up desperate to share in this moment of triumph in the presence of the sharp-suited Neil Kinnock, but significantly not that of the donkey-jacketed Michael Foot.

Likewise, the choice of the People's Palace, the Royal Festival Hall's restaurant, as the place to deliver his Dome speech the following February, in which he went to extraordinary lengths to turn around the public perception of the project. This, after all, was the place in which he first savoured the sweetness of victory. This was the last legacy of the Festival of Britain, with which Peter Mandelson's grandfather had been so closely associated. And the restaurant's name itself, despite its embrace of coriander and New World Chardonnay, is an echo of a very different kind of politics, yet one which Blair still seeks to tap.

This was a critical moment for a project that was seemingly reeling from a series of hammer blows: constant cost escalation; the news that signalling systems on the vital new Jubilee Line Extension would not be ready in time; and a House of Commons committee investigation that had voiced damaging questions about the expertize of the

entire organization. Keith Bales, who had worked for Disney, pointed out to Gerald Kaufman that, 'none of the board or the senior management of the Millennium Experience had ever run, managed, designed or promoted in any way whatsoever a major international leisure attraction'.

The Dome had faced the resignation not just of its mercurial creative director Stephen Bayley, appointed to fill the gap left by Gary Withers, but also of Erik Sorensen, the respected chief executive of the Millennium Commission who would eventually have had to stand as guarantor to the project. There was also the departure of Cameron Mackintosh, who had previously been touted as one of the jewels in the creative crown of the project. Even Peter Mandelson seemed to be losing his touch. In July 1997 he had described PVC-coated polyester as the safest and most environmentally sound fabric available for the Dome. A month later, he had authorized an

2 February 1998

1 April 1998

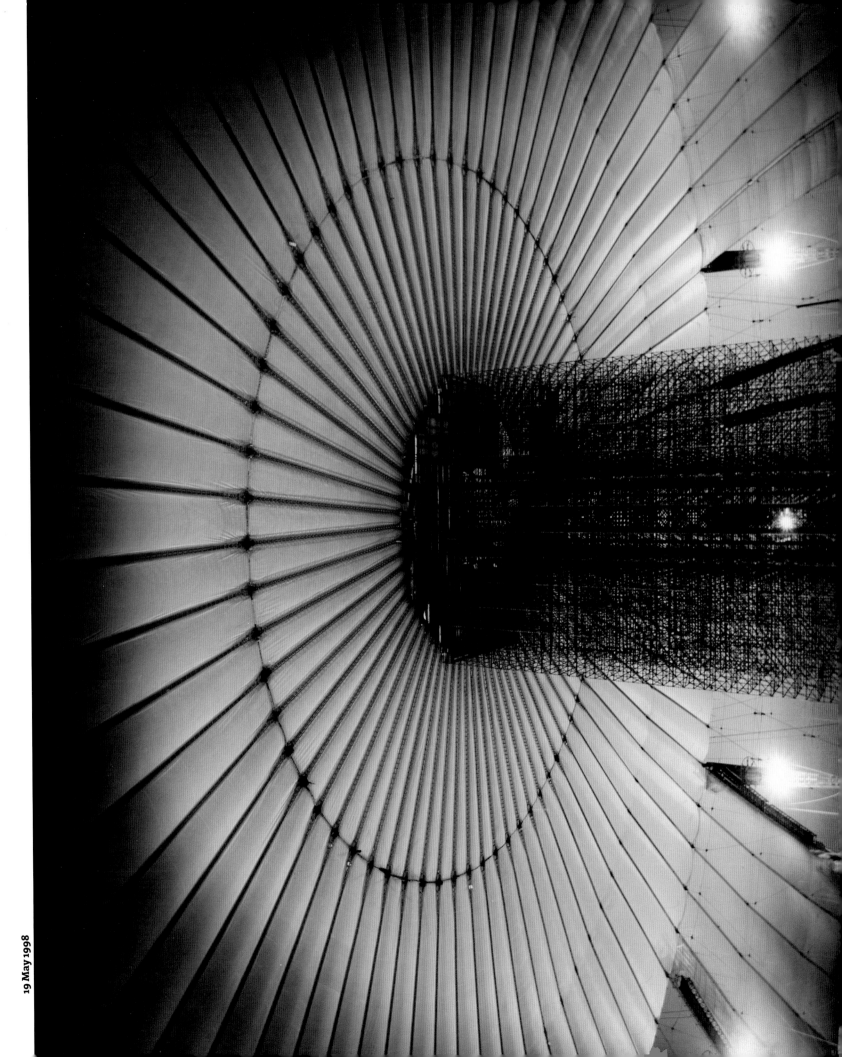

7 June 1998

The preliminary proposals for the interior, unveiled by Tony Blair, showed the intention to be both educational and entertaining. The Learning Curve (left). Serious Play (below).

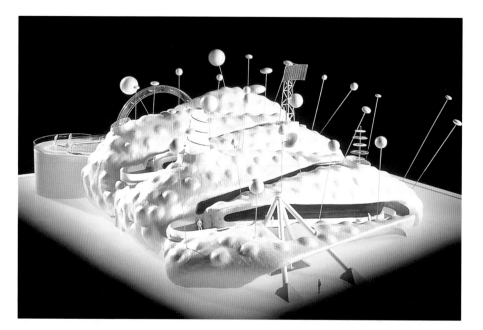

additional expenditure of £8 million to use Teflon-coated fibreglass instead.

Tony Blair's People's Palace speech was a chance to turn around perceptions of a project that appeared as if it was heading for disaster. It was a time for oratory. And Blair responded as only he knows how: 'Picture the scene. The clock strikes midnight on 31 December 1999. The eyes of the world turn to the spot where the new Millennium begins – the Meridian Line at Greenwich. This is Britain's opportunity to greet the world with a celebration that is so bold, so beautiful, so inspiring that it embodies at once the spirit of confidence and adventure in Britain and the spirit of the future in the world. This is the reason for the Millennium Experience. Not a product of the imagination run wild, but a huge opportunity for Britain. It is good for Britain. So let us seize the moment and out on something of which we and the world will be proud.

'Then we will say to ourselves with pride: this is *our* Dome, *Britain's* Dome, and believe me, it *will be* the envy of the world.

'It does not surprise me that the cynics have rubbished the idea. They are in good company. They are part of an inglorious strand of British history: like those who said St Paul's would be a calamity, that the 1851 exhibition would have no visitors and that the 1951 Festival of Britain would never be finished on time.

'It's easy to say don't do something. To say it won't be done on time. That it costs too much. That no one will visit it. It takes little courage to say no to a new idea. But just suppose we gave in to the cynics and snipers. Suppose for a second we allowed pessimism to drive out ambition. Suppose we tore down the masts, suppose we said no to the jobs and the tourists, suppose we sacked the builders and returned the land to its previous contaminated state, suppose we dismissed Britain's finest designers,

musicians, directors and singers, suppose we told Richard Rogers not to build this great building in this country, but to move it elsewhere, then when the eyes of the world fell on Greenwich people would see a derelict site and a signpost in the ground reading "Britain – year 2000. Nothing doing". Wouldn't those same cynics feel just a bit unsettled? Wouldn't they feel that Great Britain had missed an opportunity?...As we approach the Millennium we can boast that we have a richness of talent in this country that is unparalleled: the finest artists, authors, architects, musicians, designers, animators, software-makers [and] scientists. We are leading the world in creativity, so why not put it on display? Why not shout about it? The Dome will be a celebration of the Best of Britain.

'The Dome's content will contain a rich texture of feelings: spiritual, emotional, fun. It will combine the best of other attractions in a unique experience. Exhilarating like Disney

World – yet different. Educational and interactive, like the Science Museum – yet different. Emotional and uplifting like a West End musical – yet different. It will be shaped by the people. Visitors from all round the world will have the time of their lives.

'The Cabinet thought long and hard and talked long and hard about whether to go ahead with the Dome. One of the clinching arguments for me came when both John Prescott and Jack Straw talked about their memories, deep and personal, of the Festival of Britain. It clearly made a huge impact on them. I want every child in Britain to be part of the Millennium Experience. This will be a celebration for the whole country. I want today's children to take from it an experience so powerful, and memories so strong that it gives them that abiding sense of purpose and unity that stays with them through the rest of their lives. Their experience is part of the Millennium Experience.'

This is ringing rhetoric indeed. Interestingly, Mike Davies, Richard Rogers' partner, and the individual who first sketched out the outline of the Dome, has equally strong memories: 'I went to the Festival of Britain aged nine. [It was] what made me want to become an architect. I was fascinated about trying to work out what made the Skylon stand up'.

But despite the lingering ghosts of Ralph Tubbs' timber Dome of Discovery and Powell and Moya's Skylon over the Greenwich peninsula that seem to haunt the Millennium Dome, we are not seeing a nostalgic evocation of the past. Or at least not a nostalgic evocation of the 1950s. The Millennium Dome takes its cue not from the 1950s, but the 1960s. It is inspired by the same fascination with scale and the positive potential of technology that shaped the Pompidou. The image to keep in mind when you try to understand it is not the Festival of Britain, but Buckminster Fuller's photomontage

bubble over Manhattan. A giant, instant, low-cost environmental quick fix.

The Dome is not really a building at all, but a shelter that covers just under a million square metres of ground, an area the size of nine Albert Halls, and is tall enough to contain Nelson's Column. In fact there was already a pre-existing structure on the site which the Dome's twin fabric skins have been trimmed to accommodate: Terry Farrell's giant cast-concrete ventilation shaft for the neighbouring Millwall Tunnel.

The Dome is so huge that it plays curious tricks of scale. From a distance it looks truly enormous, like an aircraft carrier moored on the river, glimpsed at the end of a terraced street. But as you move closer, its absence of detail somehow makes it shrink until the point that you emerge from under its skirt, and the structure, 380 metres (1,250 feet) across, explodes overhead, leaving the viewer feeling like an ant on a bench.

It is conceived not as traditional architecture but as a means of providing the maximum shelter for the minimum cost. In these terms there can be no doubt that the Dome is brilliantly successful. The figure for the cost of the Millennium Experience is always quoted as £758 million, a sum that would buy no less than five new Tate Galleries of Modern Art. But the cost of the Dome itself is less than £60 million. As Davies points out, this is the amount that the people who build those enormous crinkly tin boxes beside motorway intersections would expect to pay for the most basic of sheds. And yet for that money Rogers has created an instantly memorable landmark, one that is powerful enough to stand its ground in a lunar landscape of gravel heaps and Thames mud. In terms of bang per buck it is unbeatable. The Dome and its 12 steel masts, as every cartoonist in Britain has discovered, is an instantly recognizable, and in the flesh, undeniably architecturally

powerful form. Indeed, it has a surprising delicacy, given that it is the product of mainly off-the-shelf components fabricated together to provide the enormous sizes that are necessary.

The Dome's design arose not from architectural heroics, but from the desire for maximum ground cover, and maximum flexibility on the site. The architects looked at alternative architectural structures to a dome, such as an asymmetric cluster of tents (something like the Munich Olympic stadium), but found it simply didn't make economic or practical sense. They looked at using a geodesic structure like the Montreal US pavilion, but it would have been hugely more expensive. Neither steel frames nor concrete shells could compete for the sheer value for money of a cable-supported tent. Though it looks all of a piece from the outside, on the inside you become aware of a more complex structural system. There

are so many structurally loaded cables that they can't be drawn altogether, but have to go into a tension ring to collect up the structural forces. The ring allows for an oculus at the top of the Dome: its centrepiece is an infill that opens to vent smoke in an emergency.

The design has been refined along the way. The masts are farther apart than they are shown in Mike Davies's original sketch. This is the result of a move to make the central space larger, which Buro Happold (responsible for the Dome's brilliant engineering) say is more efficient structurally, as well as aesthetically. The Dome is, in the words of its architects, 'simple, cheerful and festive, rather than refined'. As Mike Davies puts it, 'This is an unusually large structure, but it is based on tried and tested subsystems used in an unusual way, that makes it more than the sum of its parts. The design is the product of a series of measured decisions, in which the rigour of construction logic

becomes absolute. The form of the Dome allows the highest repetition possible. It is made up of six identical sets of systems, that work almost like spinning a suspension bridge, but with an added third dimension.'

The masts, each twice the height of Nelson's column, are awesome. Inside each of them is a huge extracting fan, bigger than a tube train. The whole structure weighs just 1,730 tonnes – a fact that Buckminster Fuller would have been delighted with, and that Mike Davies is always ready to remind us.

The Dome itself may be gossamer light, but the structural load means up to 1,000 tonnes punching weight concentrated at the foot of each of the masts, so load-spreading over the mud on which the Dome sits is essential. Thus the masts are hoisted up out of the way of pedestrians to sit on steel tripods, each of them with its own concrete foot.

Not only is the cover offered by the Dome cheap, but it allowed the organizers the time they desperately

needed to develop their ideas as to what should actually go on inside the Dome. It bought them another 12 months, without which the project simply couldn't have happened. The original idea from Gary Withers had been to build 12 distinct pavilions like a traditional expo site. The Rogers scheme was the only practical way of having the project open on time. It turned the content into exhibition fitting-out work, not civil engineering or architecture. It has been argued that the Dome should never have been conceived as a temporary structure – in which case different decisions would have been taken about materials, and possibly even about size – but given what the architects were actually asked to do, there is no doubt that they have succeeded brilliantly.

Actually it is better than that. Nobody ever articulated what was needed: a giant value-for-money, completely flexible structure that nevertheless had an instant presence. The Rogers office rose to the occasion unbidden. And with its

twin skins of Teflon-coated fibreglass – that control the climate of the interior, held up by the spider's web of cables, and lashed down by a second web of internal cables – they have done so gracefully and beautifully.

Of course, the question that must be asked is, what is it all for? What is the Dome saying about us? Tony Blair is not François Mitterrand, a politician who had enough of his own firmly developed architectural tastes to commission I. M. Pei to design the Louvre Pyramid, to decide against Future Systems as the architects of the new French library, and to take the decisions about the Grande Arche at La Défense himself. The British government is taking advice from just about everyone about the content of the Dome: from Alan Yentob of the BBC and Christopher Frayling of the Royal College of Art to David Putnam and Doris Lockhart Saatchi. And it has also brought in an enormously catholic range of designers to wrestle with the thankless task of

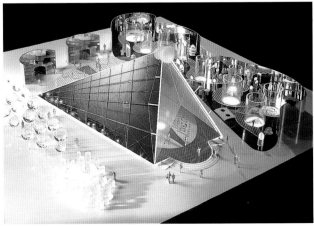

Dreamscape, where people are to travel through imaginary landscapes on giant beds (left). The Spirit Zone, the site of much agonizing over religious matters (below).

producing something worthwhile to put in it – from the commercial and the acknowledged crowd-pleasers, to the most intellectually demanding. Peter Mandelson said, when he assumed responsibility for the project in June 1997, that he was worried by the 'apparent absence of any idea of what will go in the Dome. There were lots of ideas bouncing around. None of them was pinned down [and] it was very much a blank sheet.' It has been equally hard to pin-down the ideas that Mandelson himself has floated about content. These have at various times included interactive screens that would allow you 'to qualify for 20 jobs you never knew existed' and an opportunity to 'play surfball, the new twenty-first century sport'. Neither of which will materialize.

Mandelson is committed to instilling a spiritual element into the Dome's contents, although Eva Jiricna, the architect hired to take on the 'Spirit Level', as this area is unfelicitiously designated, has struggled to square the circle of an exhibition that intends to celebrate 2,000 years since the birth of Christ without offending anybody. In the process, designers have come and gone. The design consultancy Spectrum have replaced David Bentheim as the designer in charge of the section on British identity, with Lorenzo Apicella leading the architecture programme. Nigel Coates, fast assuming the role Hugh Casson played in 1951, has struggled with the gender of the giant figure or figures that will form the centrepiece of the interior. Mark Fisher, the architect responsible for the sets used by the Rolling Stones on tour is the sensible replacement for Cameron Mackintosh, appointed when it finally became apparent that Mackintosh's idea of building a temporary theatre that could seat 10,000 simply didn't make financial sense. Zaha Hadid has clung on to a slice of the interior. MUF, the eccentrically named all-female architectural practice that is much fancied in some avant-garde circles, has not.

As Gerald Kaufman put it in his report to Parliament, 'The millennium is not just an arbitrary collection of digits, but a moment in time which has meaning not only for Christians but for everybody. It provides a great opportunity for a national celebration.' He and his committee are satisfied that the Dome itself is 'magnificent in conception, and likely to be breathtaking in execution'. They go on to say that its success 'will depend crucially upon its contents'. At the time of his investigations in December 1997, Kaufman wrote, 'The process of discovering the proposals for the content of the Dome was akin to drawing teeth. The Millennium Experience Company knows what will be in the Dome but cannot tell us. From what we know so far, the Millennium Experience is not so much a journey through time, as at any rate, for those of us who are not privy to the plans, a journey into the unknown.'

In retrospect, it is clear that at that time the Millennium Experience Company, and its sole shareholder, Peter Mandelson, didn't know what was going to be in the Dome either. The fact that on the day it opens at the end of 1999 it will contain a remarkable array of material is testimony to the fact that such giant undertakings are no longer the preserve of any single individual. For better or worse, the Dome has certainly succeeded in the overwhelming objective of Tony Blair: the creation of a single focus that sums up the achievements of his period in office. But in the sharpest of ironies, it is now clear that its ultimate reception will rest not so much on its content, symbolic or otherwise, but on the record in the real world of that government. Tony Blair was clearly persuaded that the Dome would reflect well on his government. But in truth, its the other way around; Blairism will reflect on the Dome. A successful Blair will mean a successful Dome. A catastrophic Blair will mean a catastrophic Millennium Experience.

The landscape park at Duisburg-Nord is the transformation of a former steelworks into a public park.

# Landschaftspark, Duisburg-Nord
## The rust belt blooms

Stefan Leppert

The park consists of a series of layers corresponding to the layers created by the engineers of the former steelworks (left).
These are connected by walkways (below).

Something is happening in the German coal and steel area: heavy industry is sounding the retreat, making way for a society of leisure, for nature and for service-sector companies. Landschaftspark Duisburg-Nord is one product of these changes.

The year 2000 is more than just another year; it is the marker of a new beginning. No other sequence of digits has prompted such reflection about humanity and the state of the world. International exhibitions also serve as a focal point for critical self-analysis: since the middle of the last century they have provided opportunities for taking stock of the technical and cultural state of an epoch and above all for looking optimistically to the future. The city of Hanover, which is hosting EXPO 2000, has adopted a global formula for survival as its motto: the triad 'Humanity, Nature, Technology' is intended to state that one cannot exist without the other and that the 'world as garden' (a familiar saying in Hanover) is

capable of survival.

Enormous effort and expense are being devoted to creating the exhibition in Hanover, changing the face of large areas of the city and raising some doubts as to whether this represents an efficient use of our resources. Meanwhile, 250 kilometres (155 miles) to the west, visitors have been able to see and experience the ideas embodied in the Hanover Expo, but in a simpler form. Without any great fuss or display, the design for a disused iron and steel works in Duisburg-Meiderich (completed in 1994) has highlighted a key phenomenon of the post-industrial age: re-use. This is what the motto 'Humanity, Nature, Technology' will mean, in real terms, in the future. As populations grow, there will be less space available for everyone.

Looking at it in these terms, the landscape architects Latz and Partner, from Kranzberg near Munich, implemented the EXPO 2000 slogan (widely celebrated as innovative) nearly ten years earlier,

with their competition design for Landschaftspark Duisburg-Nord. Now, large sections of their design, devised for gradual realization, have been completed: some 200 hectares (490 acres) of the former Thyssen steelworks have been given a unique new meaning.

Humanity, Nature, Technology. Humanity is placed first, for obvious reasons. The traces of human occupation are clearly apparent in Germany's Ruhrgebiet region. Consequently, there is a great need for open space, where some 30 communities and small towns grew together to form a huge residential and economic conglomeration between 1870 and 1920. It was during these years that the concept of the *Volkspark* (or national park) came into being – yet in the Ruhrgebiet the population was so dense that this concept had little impact. Over the last few years the *Volkspark* idea has again resurfaced, to popular approval. Yet new meanings must be found for these open spaces now that

fundamental elements of social and economic life have changed. Economic prosperity is no longer inextricably tied to land ownership. As we move from an industrial to a service society, huge former industrial sites are reverting from private to public ownership, and land that was formerly closed off is now accessible to everyone, a change representative of the Ruhrgebiet region.

The citizens of Meiderich accepted and adopted their new landscape park at competition stage in 1991, long before its official opening. Indeed, this fitted perfectly with the planning principle of step-by-step development adopted by Latz and Partner: the problems inherent in the site were far too complex to be eradicated completely within the three years in between winning the competition and the park's completion. The blast furnace with its associated areas and factory buildings had to be inspected for

The rail harp, a collection of sloping and curved embankments that originally carried railway tracks (above).

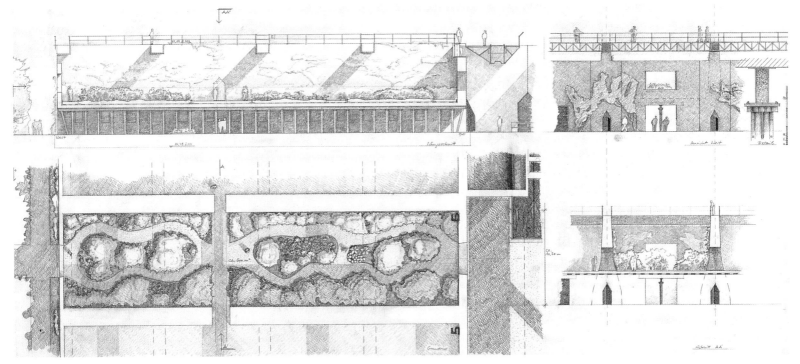

Former storage bunkers now contain courtyard gardens reached through new openings in their concrete walls.

Cowper Place is a tree-filled public space created within the old blast-furnace plant.

Rainwater is collected through existing pipe systems and allowed to fall into basins, thereby becoming enriched with oxygen (below).

potential dangers and made safe, and contaminated sections had to be temporarily closed off. A colossal amount of preparatory work was undertaken before visible work could even begin.

Despite the decline in industry, the people of the Ruhrgebiet are still 'workers', even if they no longer have any work, or if they now sell computers rather than produce steel. They are closely bound in with the traditions that made the Ruhrgebiet great and do not want to disown the heritage their predecessors worked so hard to achieve. The planners and the state-owned development company that commissioned the project acknowledged these important connections: aspirations feed on memories and public acceptance can only be achieved by establishing a connection with the past. The guiding principles were preservation, development and interpreting the legacy of the past.

The landscape architects implemented this maxim throughout, beginning at the entrance area where they fixed the regularly spaced trees not to spruce stakes but to sections of rusty steel. Visitors are able to access parts of the steel plant by walking step by step through a complex metal construction (the original plant) to a height of about 50 metres (500 feet). On the way up through the plant, there are a few information desks that explain how the plant functioned. Contrasting with the history of the site are excellent views of the still live industry of the region, situated a few kilometres away: the Landschaftspark is not just a museum of the past, it is also a piece of contemporary reality. As visitors look back towards the park, their gaze encompasses birches and poplars, which are growing up among the steel girders and ventilation towers. For the continuation of the tour, Latz and Partner have designed a long and a short route through the park. Visitors can cross the site diagonally over raised steel footbridges and look down on the former ore bunkers of the sinter plant from above. These walled pockets have been planted in a variety of ways but all have been instilled – through walls, a closed atmosphere, silence and restrained planting – with the atmosphere of a monastery garden. From here, visitors pass by the huge stock bunkers of the blast furnace, which are lined with gravel – their 12-metre- (40-foot-) high walls are now used by the local mountaineering club as a practice site. Alternatively, visitors can take the longer route, crossing over the Alte Emscher, an open waste-water sewer that is currently being converted to piping. This was not previously possible due to the landslips caused by the mines, which would have caused repeated and inaccessible leaks in the pipelines. North of the straight course of the Emscher is a large open area, partly paved over, partly covered with natural vegetation, and partly planted with rows of shrubs. Different views of the site can be seen from steel scaffolding (accessible to visitors) and from a slag heap on the park's eastern border. It is only from here that you can see the full extent of the blast furnace building, which forms an incredible backdrop.

Landschaftspark Duisburg-Nord probably offers a wider variety of attractions than any other park in Europe. Children can play in fantasy worlds, divers can disappear into underground lakes and music and theatre groups can perform against the backdrop of the decaying steel works. It is a unique world: the rusting steel plant provides a reminder of the past, while the growing trees and plants offer a thrilling sign of the future to come. Humanity, Nature, Technology. Nature is gaining ground, an industrial biotope is evolving. Birches grow best here, already covering a third of the total area and ousting increasing numbers of other plant species. In the long term, they will have to be cleared in some areas to prevent the park

A concrete theatre, coloured with recycled brick chippings, has been created in the former sintering works (left).

Gardens in the former coke and ore storage bunkers (below). Views in from a high-level walkway are created by cutting windows in the 1.2-metre- (3.9-foot-) thick walls (facing page).

The Piazza Metallica is paved with 49 iron plates, formerly used to cover casting moulds in the pig-iron casting works, and eroded by the 1600°C temperature of the process (previous page).

turning into woodland. The park's aesthetic appeal lies precisely in the interplay of different types of area: some built-up and open, some without plant covering, areas with some plants and areas rich with vegetation. Environmentalists are concerned about the birches, poplars and brambles on the one hand and about the large numbers of neophytic species on the other. Around 200 species should be growing here, yet biological succession is progressing faster than the biologists of Duisburg's Green Areas Department had anticipated. In only five years, for example, softgrass areas have developed into the beginnings of a birch forest. Controlled development will be necessary: in some areas, plants will be left to pursue their natural competition undisturbed; in others, human intervention will restrain the most aggressive species. However, biologists consider that there is no reason for panic-mongering from the environmental protection

groups who organize nature tours of the site. Industrial wasteland is a unique kind of natural environment, where cosmopolitan species such as as *Seneccio inacquidens*, *Buddleia davidii* and *Solidago canadensis* can also be tolerated. The same is true of the many 'archeophytic' species – the plants that were introduced to northern and central Europe in Roman times. Cultivated species are a third group being observed by botanical experts, who are discovering ever more species of saxifrage or physalis, which have migrated into this unfamiliar world from nearby gardens.

Humanity, Nature, Technology. An unfamiliar world. Wherever technology has taken over people and the landscape, creating an industrial wasteland, once-familiar surroundings become strange. This is particularly the case when the changes are anchored in the consciousness, even though they cannot be seen, as with the extreme soil contamination in some areas of

the park. Plants serve as an indicator of soil contamination – at least this is what common sense, not to mention plant experts, would expect. The reality has made the results of the site mapping all the more surprising: there was no clear connection between the level of contamination and the nature of the vegetation growing on an area. Everything seems to grow just as well, or just as badly, in all areas of the site. The only decisive factors appear to be the supply of nutrients and water – not, for example, the high levels of arsenic and cadmium in the area immediately around the steelworks or the aromatic hydrocarbons of the coking plant. One area, however, is completely free of vegetation and this is unlikely to change in the near future. Not a single seed will sprout in the *Teersee* (or 'tar lake'), a muddy pond that was once used to wash out the tank wagon, due to its high levels of benzol and phenol. Apart from this area, most of the park has relatively low contamination levels,

in so far as this can be said of any area within the Ruhrgebiet.

The vegetation may yield little information about the soil chemistry, but it does show where physical alterations have been made to the underlying ground, revealing traces of the past. Particular types of plant grow on former rail tracks, for example, highlighting the course they took, even though the tracks have now been removed or covered over with soil. A number of different routes come together at the *Gleisharfe* (or 'harp junction'), a distinctive landscape feature with tracks leading alternately to upper and lower levels. The industrial engineers of the past constructed this for functional, logistical reasons; now engineers have given it new life as a landscape sculpture. The rail system of the steelworks gave Peter Latz the idea of using steel footbridges to access different parts of the park. Now visitors follow the tracks formerly used only by goods wagons. These blue or pale

One garden is created with vegetation from the rail harp: birchwood is overgrown with ferns and climbers (previous page). The Piazza Metallica is used for public events (left).

The 'Ascent to the Alpine Pasture', an imaginary mountain slope for children (above). The relics of steelworks are used as climbing walls by mountaineers (facing page).

green, 250-metre- (820-foot-) long bridges run just above ground level, offering impressive views over the site and the steelworks, and into small gardens, creating another level of experience alongside the base level of the park, the underground pools, the blast furnace and the slag heap. Latz made good use of the surprise element, which this complex site possesses in abundance.

At the end of the walk the visitor re-enters a steel world made of pipes, ventilation towers, walls, stairways and railings, arriving at the 'Piazza Metallica', a square located at the heart of the blast furnace site. Here, Latz had 49 square cast-iron panels, each weighing 8 tonnes, transported from the foundry to create a unique artefact and symbol: what once covered the casting bed and existed solely for the purpose of production now functions as a work of art. However, like many of the artefacts in the park, the Piazza Metallica is also subject to a constant process of

change in which people play an active part. Events and festivals are held on the rusting panels, children play on them, water collects on them and moss grows on them. Humanity, Nature, Technology. Even though steel is no longer produced here, the world of technology can be seen everywhere.

Weekend visitors who remain until dusk can experience the surprise of a live theatrical display: as night falls, and the gigantic rusty structure begins to fade into darkness, it becomes a projection screen for 400 lights. The former gasometres are lit up symbolically in blue, the tapping plant in red and the chimneys are crowned with a yellow ring. The light display gradually builds up in 15-minute intervals, then stays at its height, and then is gradually reduced again, remaining unlit for 15 minutes. The full sequence is repeated twice each evening. Jonathan Park – an English stage designer who has worked for the Rolling Stones, Tina Turner and

Whitney Houston – created this brilliant weekend landmark in the autumn of 1996; it matches the design of the park perfectly. On this site a strong impact can only be achieved through an unambiguous but restrained design. The lighting display presents a gentle interplay rather than a noisy spectacle.

There still seems to be plenty of space at Landschaftspark Duisburg-Nord. Media professionals, concert organizers and camera teams are constantly finding new ways of using it to give shape to their ideas. The owners have decided to focus the cultural events on the steelworks and to leave other areas in peace. Ursula Poblotzki, a professor of landscape architecture, wrote in the journal *Topos* that Duisburg was a model for the *Volkspark* of the future: she may well be right. Here the past has been transformed into the present, without destroying the one or compromising the other. A former industrial world has been transformed into a play area for

children and adults. Large numbers of visitors offer proof of the park's success, and the mix of visitors it attracts is especially significant: it is no coincidence that many older people, young people, women and immigrants come to the park: these are the groups who tend not to have cars and need access to open spaces close to their homes. For many of them, a walk in the park is an escape, and in this respect the park fulfils the function of a *Volkspark*. The reason for the need to escape has changed radically since the 1920s, however: once people wanted to escape to a natural setting to breathe fresh air, now people often want to escape the bright, shrill, fast-paced world of today's service-based society. Here, the designers have created an alternative world, determined by neither stasis nor speed but by a steady to-and-fro of people, nature and technical achievements.

*Translated from the German by Susan Mackervoy*

# Shopping

Ontario Mills is a 200,000-square-metre (2-million-square-foot) retail shed, enlivened by references to California's past, such as the Mission-style cupola (opposite).

# Ontario Mills, California
## Castle of consumption in the empire of signs

Aaron Betsky

The Ontario Mills shopping mall is the strange attractor in the world of near chaos composing the sprawl of southern California. It sits like an almost – but not quite – brown blob next to a freeway interchange, huddled under the nearly vertical San Gabriel mountains, the youngest peaks in the United States. Its shape is difficult to distinguish from the massive trucking trans-shipping buildings across the freeway: 200,000 square metres (2 million square feet) of fully air-conditioned space shelters under the smog of Ontario. Inside, almost 20 million people a year lap around the Möbius strip of 'off-price retailers' in a ritual of shopping, seeing and being seen. They represent 27 different ethnic groups in the mall's catchment area. This is the place where those millions are building a community in and through consumption. The colours and heraldic signs that hold together this monument to our consumer culture are the fragments of advertising, abstractions from the area's heritage and the rhythms of light, colour and form that draw the visitor on from store to store. Ontario Mills is the monument to the new America.

Ontario Mills is the latest in a series of super malls developed by the Mills Corporation, which opened to the public in 1996, after a three-year construction and planning process. Beginning with Potomac Mills, outside Washington, DC, the Mills Corporation has developed Sawgrass Mills in Fort Lauderdale, Florida and Gurnee Mills, near Chicago, Illinois. Each one of these retail temples arranges large stores that specialize in offering goods at a discount into what used to be called an outlet mall. Now, these regional centres have replaced the traditional shopping mall as the primary destination point of many who otherwise do their upscale shopping in rehabilitated downtowns or from catalogues. The Mills Corporation attracts the hordes not just through the presence of these big-box retailers, but by packaging these packagers in an environment that gives one a sense of inhabiting a – however artificial – place in what is usually the middle of nowhere.

These are not just places in which to purchase: they are places for personal entertainment, where you can associate yourself with part of a tribe, not because of your ethnic background, but through the retailers you frequent, the music you listen to, or the sexual activity you enjoy. At the Mills projects, giant hybrids between restaurants, amusement arcades and themed environments such as Dale & Busters, Sega Gameworks, Rainforest Café and the American Wilderness Experience supplement the stores, merging a promenade through different scenes in which you play an active (and sometimes violent) role with the retail experience. Outside the actual mall, a total of 50 cinema screens draw as many as 4,000 people at a time to Ontario Mills. Over 1 per cent of *Titanic*'s opening day gross came from these screens.

What is Ontario Mills, beyond a phenomenon? What is the form of this new mammoth temple to Mammon? It is a box, of course, but one with particular characteristics. According to Henry Beer, a graduate of the Eames office and the managing partner of Boulder-based Communications Arts, the firm

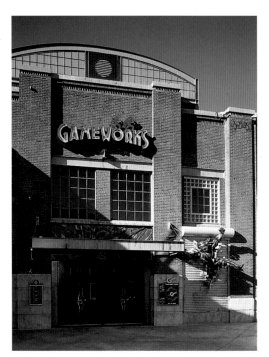

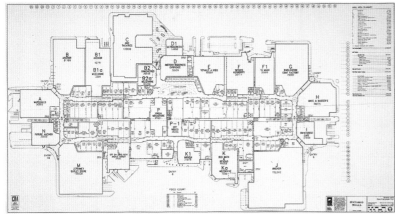

responsible for the design of the actual building (and its stores: the Mills Corporation builds most of the spaces for its tenants), the designers engage in a game of mathematics, where minimum financial resources result in maximum diversity, a visual environment and a heterogeneous place with modest materials that can be approved by the mall's funding sources. The goal, Beer says, is 'to connect our clients to their resident culture. We don't do theming; that's something I consider downstream from having ideas. We'd rather attempt to hold a mirror to a place, to give value to the shopping experience, but not in a pedagogical way. This is not much different from what buildings have always done in terms of providing the content to the functions they contain. We're like the broadcasting system of this mall, dedicated to creating a visual narrative that holds together images that come straight from advertising.'

Beer sees the worlds of projected and printed images merging with those of constructed forms, so that the advertisement a viewer sees on television or in a magazine continues into the store environment and then becomes the clothes they can wear. All the designer does is to provide a structure or rhythm to this process of natural consumption. Beer hopes their design will offer an alternative to the context provided by The Gap, Nike or Virgin Records. Architecture will continue to be not just that which a client demands, but something that gives shape to client, user and maker in a symbiotic creation.

In the case of Ontario Mills, Beer had originally intended to tie the mall down to what he saw as the

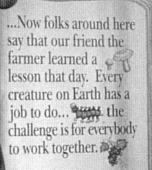

...Now folks around here say that our friend the farmer learned a lesson that day. Every creature on Earth has a job to do... the challenge is for everybody to work together.

**Under the Magic Grapevine, children can sit on toadstools. Coloured patterns, as much as historic references, are used to draw in shoppers (overleaf).**

four heritages of southern California: the Spanish missions; the City Beautiful and utopian movements that molded many of southern California's early towns (including Ontario); the beach culture; and agriculture. The city of Ontario, however, felt this model was too exclusive, and now there are ten entries into the different neighbourhoods of the mall, each one with a slightly different theme. There is a giant grapevine, a turret recalling the turn-of-the-century invention of a Spanish past known as the mission style, and a classical cupola that Beer jokingly refers to as 'the Palace of the Legion of Shoppers'. These moments of direct reference or representation are few, however. More common are the fields of muted colours that rise and fall along the walls in geometries that are never complete. These fragments swell into welcoming forms at the entrances, rise up to draw viewers on, and recede under the next layer of colour fields as the consumer moves into another section of the mall.

These colours hide the fact that the mall is essentially a block of space with no order, no punctuation and little variety. It is a self-enclosed system, with no dead ends. Only a few signs peak up above the uniform parapet height of 6.7 metres (22 feet), and a few desultory lines of palm trees are all that mark the entrances in a larger landscape. Inside, there is only the march of storefronts, though at certain times wood floors (a Mills Corporation specialty) give way to concrete and even carpet, while skylights punctuate the metal ceiling. Servicing runs though a tunnel down the middle of the structure. Signage is all, since the physical

envelope is so rudimentary that it fades into the background.

In the food court, those signs take on form. There, the giant letters naming the space hang at an angle over the rows of stalls. Their bulbous forms join balloons that resemble, Oldenburg-like, the hamburgers and fries one can buy from the many stalls lining the space. This court was originally supposed to be a food hall with a soaring roof, but cost concerns drove the ceiling down to the level of the rest of the mall experience, heightening the sense of a scale shift as consumers huddle under the pop art abstractions of their consumption. All the food outlets are run by the same company, so that the taco maker can quickly become a Starbucks barrista.

There is a method to this seeming miasma. What Communications Arts and the Mills Corporation have done is to take some of the central building types of Western culture to their logical extreme. Ontario Mills of course has its roots, like all malls, in the crystal palaces that arose in the late-nineteenth century. These havens of glass and steel democratized the riches previously reserved for the aristocracy under structural webs that did away with the fancy dress of old palaces. The dissolution of fixed forms in favour of open space and reflective surfaces highlighted the merchandising and made these department stores and galleries into emblems of the wealth and the mobility of the middle classes and their condition, modernity.

By the middle of the twentieth century, the shopping mall had both perfected and simplified this model into a world of complete transparency hovering inside

boxes. Those efficient constructions did away with most attempts to locate themselves in time and space through façades or other forms of clearly articulated appearance. The mall lost the look of a palace and took on the character of an assembly hall: large, simple-span single-level structures surrounded by acres of parking. The optimum amount of goods and people could gather here. The stucco enclosures of these buildings were, and are, flexible in their arrangements and use the least amount of structure possible. They create a completely free and functional space, which, moreover, is completely artificial, as it is cut off from external reality – including outside views and air.

Previously, malls tried to hide these developments. The Mills, whose name alone recalls a factory, prides itself on its quasi-industrial nature. The articulation that architects impose on forms is, after all, a luxury that must eventually be passed on to the consumer in the price of the object they buy. Here at the Mills, this luxury has made way for the simple appearance of the object itself, which is now presented as shorn of pretensions. One can easily see the trusses, the brown stucco walls and the concrete that goes into making the place, but one does not notice it, because the sign takes over.

This is all that is left: signage. Here the third element in Ontario Mills' heritage reveals itself. It is a scaffolding for signs that – like in a world's fair, an exhibit or any other form of framing – highlights and gives an aura to the objects it contains. This is a cathedral to commerce that borrows as much from the ways in which statues and sacred rhythms reinforce ritual as it

does from the rollercoaster rides of entertainment parks. Finally, the designers have almost dissolved the scaffolding into the invisible mechanics of projected reality. The Mills' collage aesthetic owes as much to the visual logic of jump cuts, swoops and pans associated with MTV as it does to the aedicule, of which John Summerson wrote so lovingly. The sign is now almost completely free from the last vestiges of form, so that Beer's merger between real and projected form can come to pass.

Ontario Mills is the perfect embodiment of the position in which architecture finds itself at the end of the millennium. It has reduced itself to an almost nothing that has freed not the individual, but the seductive image, to float in front of us at will. We, meanwhile submit ourselves to a structure defined not by columns and enfilades, but by the logic of economics (what we can afford, which spaces we control) hiding behind the shimmering veils of ever-changing fashion that keeps the engine of production and consumption humming along.

What remains to architecture are two things: its character – that which creates a relationship between ourselves as bodies (objects) and subjects and the world we inhabit – and its similar function in time. (We want to have one foot in nostalgia and one foot in prophecy, says Beer, quoting the author Frederick Morton discussing *fin-de-siècle* Vienna in *Thunder at Twilight*.) In the case of Ontario Mills, these roles lack the high-minded appearance of architecture, like Bernard Tschumi's event structures, or the elitist re-interpretation that engages Robert

Venturi and Denise Scott-Brown. Instead, Communication Arts presents architecture as an act of editing, abstracting and sequencing that which already exists in such a way that it makes sense of itself and the culture in which it appears – more like collage artists for whom meaning appears in the act of collecting and the relationships that composed fragments establish with each other and the viewer.

In the case of Ontario Mills, the building is so much a mirror that it shimmers almost to the point of disappearing. As one drops down in an airplane or cruises in a car into the haze that spreads throughout the Inland Empire, as the region around Ontario calls itself, the off-browns and ochres of the Mills building appear like slight solidifications of that air itself. Their pale puce, purple and yellow accents seem like man-made versions of the hues that wash over the semi-arid terrain itself. Their punctuation comes not from seasonal wild flowers, but from the changing colours of advertising.

The form of the building is a coalescence of the gated communities that surround the Mills. There, hundreds of individual dwellings hover together behind equally blank walls. Across the freeway, tilt-up concrete warehouses store goods and people without giving any hint of the riches or space they contain. Office buildings, hospitals and jails continue the horizontal enclosures into banded, pale-coloured boxes that give little hint on the outside of what they contain. The Mills project is merely the biggest and

densest of all these forms.

What gives it character is its identity system: the signage, advertising and 'wayfinding' systems that Communication Arts has provided. Just as trees and vegetation mark the courses of the waterways that are so rare in this area, so signage follows the freeways and arterial boulevards, clumping up around the interchanges that act as wells of motion and capture capital before it moves on to its next investment. The Ontario Mills project is one of the largest of such oases of signs. It has sprouted at the place where the great road west intersects the road that leads down from the still empty high desert, between the San Bernardino and San Gabriel mountain ranges, and along the Interchange 15 Strip that is the latest frontier of development.

Ontario Mills is the condensation of this landscape. Its forms are not only the most expedient enclosures possible, but also the solidification of its context in both time and space. The former dimension comes in through the references to the past forms of buildings that once dotted this valley. They mix with the neon, the large televisions suspended inside the mall, the virtual reality rides and the digital output signs that dot the storefronts. It all comes together at this point.

The only thing lacking is content. The medium has finally become the message, or rather, the reverse: Ontario Mills is a system of inhabited signs. We ritualistically drive around and perambulate through markers of time and place, trying to assimilate advertising that has

solidified in goods. We consume, and in the act we define ourselves. If there is a melting pot here in the Inland Empire, says Beer, then this is that vessel. It all comes together not in shared ideals, but in the act of shopping. If we can suspend, even for one moment, our judgement about whether we want a commercial enterprise to control the forging of identity, without worrying about the environmental impact of the mall, we can admire the skill and completeness it represents.

The architect Victor Gruen, whom many credit with having invented the shopping mall, gave the world of economics and real estate one of the few phrases named after an architect: the Gruen Transfer. This is the moment when, due to the complexity of the shopping mall, the directed shopper who came for a particular purchase is distracted, loses their way and starts wandering. In reproducing the nomadic existence that seems proper to the ex-urban resident (and to the capital that feeds sprawl), the Gruen Transfer is the moment of the birth of a new kind of space. It is the moment also when previous criteria for architecture stops making sense, as do many ethical and moral judgements. Here, architecture becomes not about defining place and thus a clear relationship to the world, but to purposefully losing one's way and dissolving into space. All we can do is to wander into Ontario Mills, find the beauties and the weirdness of this enigmatic empire of consumption, and erect new judgements proper to its peculiar almost-forms.

# Project credits

**The Tate Gallery of Modern Art, London**
*Architect*
Herzog & de Meuron
*Associate Architect*
Sheppard Robson
*Landscape Architect*
Kienast Vogt
*Engineer*
Ove Arup & Partners
*Building Project Managers*
Stanhope
*Construction Manager*
Schal
*Cost Consultant*
Davis, Langdon and Everest

**Berlin: The Jewish Museum**
*Client*
Senatsverwaltung für Bauen, Wohnen
und Verkehr, Berlin
*User*
The Jewish Museum, Berlin
*Architect*
Daniel Libeskind, Berlin
*with Project Architect*
Matthias Roese and Jan Dinnebier

*Primary consultants*
*Landscape Architect*
Müller, Knippschild, Wahberg, Berlin
*Civil Engineer*
Cziesielski + Partner, Berlin
*Structural Engineer*
GSE Tragwerkplaner, Berlin and IGW
Ingenieurgruppe Wiese, Berlin

*Special Consultants*
*Cost and Site Control*
Arge Beusterien und Lubio, Berlin
*Lighting*
Lichplanung Dinnebier KG, Wuppertal

**Potsdamer Platz**
*Master Plan*
Renzo Piano Architects' Co-operative
Christoph Kohlbecker
*General supervision and building
management*
debis Gesellschaft für Potsdamer Platz
Projekt und
Immobilienmanagement mbh
*General Manager*
Drees & Sommer AG
*Architects of individual buildings*
Renzo Piano and Christoph Kohlbecker;
associate architect Bernard Plattner
Arata Isozaki and Associates with Steffen
Lehmann & Partner
Hans Kollhoff
Ulrike Lauber and Wolfram Wöhr
José Rafael Moneo
Richard Rogers Partnership

**The Reichstag**
*Architects*
Foster and Partners
*Client*
Federal Republic of Germany represented
by Bundesbaugesellschaft Berlin mbH

*Consultants*
*Structural Engineer*
Ove Arup & Partners
Schlaich Bergermann & Partner
Leonhardt Andrä & Partner
*Mechanical, Electrical and Environmental
Services*
Kaiser Bautechnik
Kuehn Associates
Fischer-Energie and Haustechnik
Amstein & Walthert
Planungsgruppe Karnasch-Hackstein
*Conservation Consultants*
Acanthus
*Quantity Surveyors*
Davis, Langdon & Everest
*Quantity Surveyor Site Supervision*
Büro Am Lützowplatz
*Acoustics*
Müller BBM GmbH
IKP, Prof. Dr. Georg Plenge
*Catering Facilities*
LZ Plan-Team
*Lifts, Materials, Handling Technology*
Jappsen & Stangier
*Lighting*
Claude & Danielle Engle
*Fire Protection*
Prof. W. Klingsch
*Cladding Consultants*
Emmer Pfenninger Partner AG

**Sony Centre**
*Owner*
Sony with its partners Tishman Speyer
and Kajima operating as BE-ST
Bellevuestrasse Development GmbH & Co.
Forst Real Estate KG
*Developer*
Tishman Speyer Properties Deutschland
GmbH
*Architect*
Helmut Jahn

**Chek Lap Kok, Hong Kong**
*Client*
Hong Kong Airport Authority

*Consultants*
*The Mott Consortium*
*Foster and Partners*
Architects and Designers
11F Guangdong Investment Tower
148 Connaught Road Central
Hong Kong
*Mott Connell Ltd*
Engineering and Project Management
40 Hopewell Centre
183 Queen's Road
Hong Kong
*BAA plc*
Airport Planning, Operational Systems
Group Technical Services
Jubilee House
Furlong Way
North Terminal, Gatwick Airport
London RH6 oJN, UK

*Other Consultants*
*Ove Arup and Partners*
Structural Engineering
56th Floor Hopewell Centre
183 Queen's Road, Hong Kong
*WT Partnership*
Cost Consultant
25/F China Overseas Building
139 Hennessy Road
Wanchal, Hong Kong
*Fisher Marantz Renfro Stone*
Architectural Lighting Design
126 Fifth Avenue
New York 10011, USA
*O'Brien-Kreizberg and Associates Ltd*
Construction Programming
*Wilbur Smith Associates*
Traffic Planning

**Yokohama International Port Terminal**
*Client*
Port and Harbour Authority and the City
of Yokohama
*Architects*
Foreign Office Architects, London:
Farshid Moussavi and Alejandro Zaera-
Polo with Kenichi Matsuzawa, Santiago
Triginer, Jordi Mansilla, Felix Bendito
*Local Architecture Consultant*
GKK Architects, Japan
*Structural Engineers*
Structural Design Group, Japan
*Mechanical and Electrical Engineers*
P. T. Morimura, Japan

**Lake Las Vegas Resort**
Developed by Transcontinental
Properties, Inc., a subsidiary of
Transcontinental Corporation, as the
developer, with entities owned by Sid and
Lee Bass of Fort Worth, Texas
*Land Planning*
Berkus Design Studios, Santa Barbara,
California
*Landscape Architecture*
Peridian International, Newport Beach,
California
Tracey & Ryder, Las Vegas, Nevada
*Architecture Control*
Berkus Design Studios, Santa Barbara,
California
*Engineers*
Kimley-Horn & Associates, Las Vegas,
Nevada
Bossard Development and Services,
Henderson, Nevada
*Interior Design*
Fielden and Partners, Las Vegas, Nevada
Sue Firestone and Associates, Santa
Barbara, California
Pollock & Associates, Costa Mesa,
California

**Gifu housing, Japan**
*Architect*
Sanaa Ltd./Kazuyo Sejima, Ryue
Nishizawa & Associates
*Client*
Gifu Prefectural Government, Japan,
Office for Social Housing
*Consultants*
O.R.S. (Structure)
Asano Setaubi (Mechanical)
Kazuyo Sejima & Associates (Architecture
Design Principal)
Usami-gumi (Construction Principal)

**Shanghai World Financial Center**
*Owner*
Forest Overseas Co. Ltd.
*Architect*
Kohn Pedersen Fox
*Architect and Engineer of Record*
Shimizu Corporation
*Project Architect and Engineer*
Mori Building Architects and
Engineers Ltd.
*Collaborative Architect*
East China Architectural Design and
Research Institute

**The Millennium Experience, London**
*Architect*
Richard Rogers Partnership
*Client*
The New Millennium Experience
Company Ltd.
*Millennium Commission*
Eric Sorensen
*Planning Supervisors*
Ove Arup & Partners
*Structural Engineers*
Buro Happold Consulting Engineers
*Steel*
Watson Steel Limited
*Fire Consultants*
FEDRA
Warrington Fire Research Consultants
*Civils & Remediates*
WS Atkins
*Construction Managers*
McAlpine Laing Joint Venture
*Environmental Engineers*
Battle McCarthy
*Quantity Surveyor*
Boyden & Co.
Gardiner & Theobald
Ove Arup & Partners
*Specification Writers*
Schumann Smith
*Health and Safety*
Health & Safety Executive
*Acoustic Consultant*
Sandy Brown Associates
*Site Photographer*
Grant Smith
*Computer Montages*
Hayes Davidson
*Modelmakers*
Millennium Models

**Landschaftspark, Duisburg-Nord**
*Client*
Development Company of Nordrhein –
Westfalen in trusteeship for the town of
Duisburg (LEG NRW)
*Landscape Architect*
Latz + Partner
*Project Team*
Latz + Partner, Kranzberg/Duisburg
Latz – Riehl, Kassel
G. Lipkowsky, Oberhausen

*Consultants*
*Structural Engineer*
Natterer + Dittrich, München
*Vegetation concept*
J. Dettmar
*Cooperating Community Groups*
Gartenamt der Stadt Duisburg (Authority
for Public Green)
Gesellschaft für Industriekultur (Society
for Industrial Culture)
IG Nordpark (Community of Interests
Nordpark)
IBA (International Building Exhibition)

Realization by help of numerous citizen
groups, employment programmes for
people out of work, workshops with
students, pupils and trainees.

**Ontario Mills, California**
*Owner/Developer*
The Mills Corporation
Larry Siegel (CEO & Chairman
of the Board)
Steven J. Jacobsen (Senior Vice President)
*Mills Development Team*
Steven Jacobsen (Senior Vice President)
James Whitcome (Senior Vice President)
Gregg Goodman (Senior Vice President/
Leasing)
Jerry Engen (Development Director)
Peter Lehrer (Senior Project Manager)
*Joint Venture Partners*
KanAm Realty
Simon Property Group
*Designer/Graphic Arts*
Communication Arts, Inc.
*General Contractor*
Whiting-Turner Contracting Company
*Production Drawings*
Feola, Carli & Archuleta Architects

# Index

# Picture credits

**Introduction**
Dennis Gilbert/View (9)
Rowan Moore (10 bottom, 11, 12, 13)
Rowan Moore (14 top and bottom right)
Photographer: Monica Nouwens (14 bottom left)
Photographer: Monica Nouwens (15)
Rowan Moore (16 top) Monica Nouwens (16 bottom)
Rowan Moore (17)
Copyright Paul Warchol (18, 19)
Joe Low/Arcaid (20 top)
Enrico Ferorelli/Colorific!(20 bottom)
Enrico Ferorelli/Cororific!(21)
Communication Arts Inc. (22 bottom)
Photographer: Timothy Hursley (23 both)
Photographer: Charles LeNoir (24-25)
Photographer: Berger-Conser (26 )
Photographer: Monica Nouwens (27 top)
Copyright Regan/Gamma Liaison/Frank Spooner
Pictures(27 bottom)
The Natural History Museum, London (28)
Mark Power/Network Photographers (28-29)
Richard Bryant/Arcaid (30)
Richard Rogers Partnership (31 top)
Rowan Moore (31 bottom)
Rowan Moore (32-33)
Edge Media, New York (35 top left)
Rowan Moore (35 top right, bottom)
Halstead/Gamma Liaison/Frank Spooner Pictures
(36 top, bottom left)
Dan Lamont/Matrix/Colorific! (36 bottom right)
David Churchill/Arcaid (37 )
Photographer: Gerald Zugmann (38)
Paul Raftery/Arcaid (39, 40-41)
Nicholas Grimshaw & Partners (42 left)
Photographer: Andrew Putler (43 top)
John Edward Linden/Arcaid (44, 45)
Dennis Gilbert/View (46)
Sony, Berlin (47 top)
Rowan Moore (47 bottom)
Courtesy Calvin Klein (48)
Seki Hirano/Architectural Association (49)
Kazuyo Sejima Associates (50 left)
Photographer: Margherita Spiluttini (51)
Photographer: Margherita Spiluttini (52-53)
Russell Bell/Wordsearch (54)
Photographer:Latz and Partners (55)
Paul Raftery-Arcaid (56-58, 58-59)

**Culture**
Photographer: Chorley Handford (60)
Photographer: Richard Glover (61)
Photographer: Marcus Leith (62)
Photographer: Margherita Spiluttini (63 both)
Photographer: Hayes Davidson (64, 64-65, 66)
Photographer: Hayes Davidson (67 top)
Photographer: Marcus Leith (67 bottom)
Russell Bell/Wordsearch (68, 69)
Herzog & de Meuron (70-71)
Photographer: Hayes Davidson (72 top)
Photographer: Marcus Leith (72-73)

**Politics**
Photographer: Richard Davies (74)
Michel Denance/Archipress (75)
Russell Bell (76)
Dennis Gilbert/View (77, 78-79)
Next Edit, Stuttgart (80 bottom)
Michel Denance/Archipress (81)
Werner Mahler/Ostkreuz (82-83)
Suzanne Hubbard/Times Newspapers Ltd (85)
Rudi Meisel/Visum (86-87, 88)
Foster and Partners (89)

**Hub space**
Foster and Partners (90)
Dennis Gilbert/View (91)
Foster and Partners (93 left)
Photographer: Richard Davies (93 top right)
Dennis Gilbert/View (94-95)
Dennis Gilbert/View (96-97 top)
Foster and Partners (96-97 middle)
Dennis Stock/Magnum (96 bottom)
Dennis Gilbert/View (97 bottom)
Foster and Partners (97 top)
Dennis Gilbert/View (98-99, 100 top)
Foster and Partners (100 bottom)
Dennis Gilbert/View (101)
Photographer: Michel Porro (102-103)
Foster and Partners (104 left)
Dennis Gilbert/View (104-105, 106 both)

**Public space**
Foreign Office Architects (106-119)

**Private housing**
Photographer: Monica Nouwens (121)
Photographer: Paul Davies (126 left)

**Public housing**
Photographer: N Nakagawa-Kazuyo Sejima
& Associates (128)
Kazuyo Sejima & Associates (129)
Photographer: N Nakagawa-Kazuyo Sejima
& Associates (130-131)
Photographer: N Nakagawa-Kazuyo Sejima
& Associates (134-135)
Kazuyo Sejima & Associates (136-137)
Kazuyo Sejima & Associates (140-141)

**Money**
Edge Media, New York (142)
Edge Media, New York (143)
Rowan Moore (144 left)
Edge Media, New York (144 right, 145)
Edge Media, New York (147, 148)
Edge Media, New York (150-151)
Edge Media, New York (154, 155 top, 157)

**Spectacle**
NMEC/Hayes Davidson/Chorley Handford (158)
Photographer: Richard Waite (159)
Mary Evans Picture Library (160, 161 left)
Hulton Getty (162 both)
Photographer: Richard Waite (163)
Mark Power/Network Photgraphers (164-173)
NMEC (174 both)
NMEC/Hayes Davidson (175, 176)
NMEC (177)

**Nature**
Photographer: Michael Latz (178)
Latz and Partners (179)
Latz and Partners (180 right)
Latz and Partners (181)
Photographer: Michael Latz (182 left)
Latz and Partners (182 right)
Photographer: Michael Latz (183, 184-185, 186 left)
Latz and Partners (186 right)
Latz and Partners (187)
Latz and Partners (188-189)
Photographer: Michael Latz (190 left)
Latz and Partners (190 right)
Latz and Partners (191)

**Shopping**
Communication Arts Inc. (192-203)